Family Life Today:
The Greatest Revolution?

Edited by Harry Bohan

VERITAS

First published 2009 by
Veritas Publications
7/8 Lower Abbey Street
Dublin 1
Ireland
Email publications@veritas.ie
Website www.veritas.ie

ISBN 978 1 84730 168 0

'Family Project' photographs © Elizabeth Handy
Cover design by AViD Graphic Design

Printed in the Republic of Ireland
by ColourBooks Ltd, Dublin

Veritas books are printed on paper made from the wood
pulp of managed forests. For every tree felled, at least one
tree is planted, thereby renewing natural resources.

Items should be returned on or before the last date shown below. Items not already requested by other borrowers may be renewed in person, in writing or by telephone. To renew, please quote the number on the barcode label. To renew online a PIN is required. This can be requested at your local library.
Renew online @ **www.dublincitypubliclibraries.ie**
Fines charged for overdue items will include postage incurred in recovery. Damage to or loss of items will be charged to the borrower.

Leabharlanna Poiblí Chathair Bhaile Átha Cliath
Dublin City Public Libraries

Dublin City
Baile Átha Cliath

Brainse Bhaile Thormod
Ballyfermot Library

Tel. 6269324/5

Date Due	Date Due	Date Due
1 9 NOV 2013		
2 3 FEB 2014		
2 4 JUL 2014		
0 5 SEP 2014		

Contents

Where Does Family Fit?

Home and School

Foreword

Fr Harry Bohan
Chairman of the Céifin Centre

A constant theme running through the ten Céifin Conferences since 1998 has been changes in family life. A key question to emerge from the first conference was 'Who is rearing the next generation?' and that question has not gone away.

There is no doubt family life has changed over the last few decades. The extent of this change is evident from the Census figures of 2006, which show a marked increase in non-traditional family patterns. The implications for society are enormous.

It was felt that the Céifin Conference of 2008 should concentrate on different aspects of family life in Ireland – it should be examined not as an argument for or against anything, but as an entity in itself. What does family life really mean to our society and what does it contribute to human, social and spiritual development?

The economic miracle from 1994–2007 brought undreamed of affluence. The Irish economy was transformed from one characterised by high levels of unemployment, high levels of government debt, forced emigration and low levels of personal debt, to an economy characterised by relatively low levels of unemployment, high levels of personal debt, low levels of government debt and strong inward migration. In many ways these developments have been very positive, but the basic nature of the population has changed dramatically.

During this period we became a nation of high spenders, high borrowers and conspicuous consumers. Nowhere is the change in the Irish psyche more apparent than in relation to foreign investment. Over the past decade we have invested heavily in bricks and mortar domestically, and when the domestic investment opportunities were exhausted, we then turned our attention to the rest of the world. The Irish have colonised the world of property and are now notorious in every city where property development occurs. This is a very dubious notoriety.

In short, greed became the all-pervasive driver of behaviour, and civilised values and a sense of community have been sacrificed on the altar of conspicuous consumption.

While we were busy with all of this and more, relationships suffered, particularly in the area of family and community. Family values now appear to be much stronger in many northern European societies and in the United States than in Ireland. Unlike many of these countries, Ireland facilitated the rampant consumerism that gripped it, with shops opening seven days per week and some twenty-four hours per day. The shopping centre became the social outlet for many families on Sunday afternoons. Financial pressures driven by the need to maintain a bloated lifestyle resulted in couples being forced to commute for hours to get to and from work. These pressures leave little time or energy for family or community life.

It is now well documented that the economy that brought about this massive material progress was underpinned by financial markets, which were completely out of control. This was obvious for a long time and yet we continued recklessly investing in a way of life that has now crashed down around us.

All of this is not to say that the economic miracle was unwelcome; it was welcomed with open arms and gave Ireland a new standing on the international scene. However, we forgot the values which underpin the priceless things in life. In short, we blew an opportunity to create the balance between economic success and a healthy family life.

The family and local community were the two systems which held Irish society together for generations. They were seriously ignored and undermined in the face of the influence of market values and the onward march of big corporations. They will once again be called on not only to cope with change, but to provide the creativity, leadership and vision for the future. Change will not now come from the top; it will come from mobilised grassroots.

The big question now is: how resourceful are family units after a period of consumerism? Can they be facilitated to make the sea change into the future?

Can community be recreated? It does not just happen, it has to be tended and fostered. Crisis underlines its importance. We do need neighbours; we came to believe we didn't.

This year we encouraged people who are very much part of families and communities, representatives from family support agencies as well as from the world of education, business, religion and the wider public to attend the conference. The family needs support – it needs the support of the community. Family formation needs to be woven into the life of every local community. This is evident from people who have been putting in place parenting and family programmes at local community level.

We were delighted at this year's conference to once again have so many young people attend, as well as parents and representatives from family support agencies.

Cardinal Brady gave the keynote address with what turned out to be a controversial paper in which he clearly outlined the Catholic Church's position regarding the family as the foundation of society.

Family Life Today: The Greatest Revolution?

Kieran McKeown, no stranger to Céifin, crucially reminded us of the importance of quality relationships at the heart of any family unit.

Charles Handy explored the impact of changing work patterns on family life and, with John Quinn, teased out what implications these changes might have on family life in the future.

California-based psychologist John Yzaguirre brought together his psychological and spiritual backgrounds to present a 'new vision' for family life. He built on this theme with his wife Claire Frazier-Yzaguirre in his workshop on day two of the conference. We were delighted to welcome them to Ireland and heartened by their positivity for the future of family life.

A highlight of the two days was the 'Telling My Story' panel discussion on family life and parenting in Ireland. Many thanks to our three panelists, Mamo McDonald, Kevin Murphy and Geraldine Reidy, who contributed to this wonderfully honest and practical discussion, focusing on the challenges faced by different generations of Irish families in bringing up their children. Thanks again to Ciana Campbell for her skilful and considerate facilitation.

Day two saw the inimitable Jim Power focus on how the economic crisis has impacted and will continue to impact on family life in Ireland. Geoffrey Shannon in his excellent presentation on where 'the family' stands in Irish Law clarified many questions thrown up over the two days.

We were delighted to welcome Marie Murray back to Céifin again, to deliver a heartfelt presentation on the real essence of where families are and how children can be best supported to create fulfilling relationships.

John Quinn brought us through Dr Patrick Hillery's many achievements when serving as Minister for Education. Hillery's long-sighted vision for Irish education and his perseverance in the face of adversity was beautifully recalled by John and acknowledged in the form of the 2008 Céifin Award, which was presented to his widow, Maeve Hillery.

Mary Forde, in the Patrick Hillery Memorial Lecture, addressed the often unseen side to Irish education today. She outlined the many pressures on parents, students and teachers, and also the steps that need to be taken to ensure greater support within the system for all stakeholders.

Huge thanks to our wonderful chair Rachael English, who continues to support Céifin with unflagging enthusiasm and professionalism.

Many thanks to all of the delegates this year for their keen interest and participation, we hope that we have provided plenty of food for thought and seeds for action!

Last but not least, we are grateful to all those who worked in the background to ensure the success of Céifin 2008: Joe Fenwick; Shannonside AV; Kate Bowe PR; and all the staff in the West County Hotel.

Dedicated members of the Céifin Board play a vital part in giving direction to the work of Céifin – we are indebted to them for their generosity with their time and talents: Bernie, Ciara and Linda in Céifin and the many loyal volunteers from RRD and all around Co. Clare, whose support is absolutely crucial, thank you all.

Fr Harry Bohan
Chairman

Family Life

The Family as the Foundation of Society

Cardinal Seán Brady
Archbishop of Armagh

'The prospect of a married couple establishing a happy, loving and stable family home in Ireland today has never been greater. Our challenge is to help women and men rediscover the joy of marriage, the life-long fulfilment it can offer, especially those who are reluctant to make a long-term commitment.' – Cardinal Brady

Introduction

It is a particular privilege to be asked to address the Céifin Conference on the tenth anniversary of its foundation in 1998. Since then it has become one of the best-known and highly respected annual events in the country. It has generated lively debate and made a very significant contribution to the important topics discussed over those ten years. I take this opportunity to congratulate Fr Harry and the others involved in founding the Céifin Conference. I salute their initiative and creativity in establishing a much-needed forum for debate during this critical period in our country's history. Long may it continue.

I am going to address the theme of 'The Family as the Foundation of Society'. There are few institutions more important to the future of our society than the family. There are few that have been subject to such rapid and fundamental change in our lifetime.

Family Life Today: The Greatest Revolution?

I would like to explore some of the contours of that change. In particular, I would like to set out the basis for the Church's conviction that marriage, the family and the general good of society are so interdependent that one cannot flourish without the other. I will examine some of the recent trends associated with marriage and the family. I will argue that legislation and policies that promote commitment in marriage are, in fact, more socially progressive and beneficial to society than those which endorse, simply because they have become more widespread, attitudes and trends which undermine that commitment. I will also comment on the question of a proposed equivalence between cohabitation and marriage as well as same-sex unions and marriage. This, as you know, has been the subject of considerable public debate in light of the government's intention to introduce new legislation in this area.

Let me share with you the contents of a letter, which may express more adequately than I ever could the essential link between faith, family and society. It is offered through the eyes and perhaps with the wisdom of an older generation. It captures something of the scale of change that has occurred in Ireland in recent years – what the title of the conference describes as a 'revolution'. It was sent to me by a seventy-seven-year-old Clare woman, now living in Kilkenny, wishing me well for my visit to her native county. She decided to write to me when she heard that I was going to talk about the family and to suggest a few ideas for my talk. Such help is always welcome! She said:

> When I grew up we never knew what money looked like, we were never hungry, we had a family life, we always said the Rosary and had time to talk with our neighbours.
> Today we have so much money that people have no time for anything, most of all God. There is no word about sin or the Ten Commandments.

There is nothing wrong today. What good is money and big houses? Do they bring happiness? All those things only last for a while. This is the only thing that lasts – God.

Please tell the people about what matters most, their souls, not their bodies. Bring back family life, family prayer and read the Bible.

Marriage and the Word of God

I was struck by this last sentence in particular. It bore a remarkable resemblance to something that was said at the recent Synod of Bishops in Rome. The theme was 'The Word of God in the Life of the Church'. Proposition 20 of the Synod spoke specifically of the link between marriage, family and the Word of God. It goes as follows:

> The Word of God stands at the origins of marriage (Gen 2:24). Jesus himself inserted marriage among the institutions of his Reign (Mt 19:4-8), giving it a sacramental status.
>
> In the sacramental celebration, man and woman pronounce a prophetic word of reciprocal donation of self, they become 'one flesh', a sign of the mystery of the union of Christ and the Church (Eph 5:32). Through the fidelity and the unity of the life as a family, the spouses are the first announcers of the Word of God to their children. It's necessary to sustain them and to help them develop within the family, modes of domestic celebration of the Word such as reading the Bible, and other forms of prayer.
>
> Spouses should recall that the Word of God is a precious source of support amid difficulties in conjugal life and in the family.

Family Life Today: The Greatest Revolution?

This brings me to my first point: the family based on marriage as the foundation of society is a truth revealed by God in the Scriptures; it is also one of the most precious human values. We should not be surprised, then, that when people become less concerned with what God has to say generally, or when the popularity of an idea replaces objective human values as the basis of morality, commitment to marriage as the basis of the family also diminishes. As the letter suggests, what we are involved in here is a wider 'revolution' about how we approach morality and values generally. So, how should we respond to this revolution? How might we invite people to rediscover the importance of the family based on marriage as the basis of society?

Changes in Attitudes to Marriage

Part of that response, I would suggest, is to acknowledge that some aspects of this so-called 'revolution' have been good for marriage and the family. While the letter I read reflects a concern that we have lost something valuable from the past, I am sure no one would want to say that everything about marriage and the family in the past was good. We should be glad, for example, that there is more equality between men and women in marriage and in society in general. There is a greater awareness that both parents have a mutual responsibility in bringing up their children and in sharing domestic tasks. We have learned so much about the importance of responding to the emotional and practical needs of children and about how to support the development of children in constructive ways. We are also learning just how important a stable family home is to the happiness and long-term well-being of children, to which I will return later.

All of this is good. In fact, I would go so far as to say that the prospect of a married couple establishing a happy, loving and stable family home in Ireland today has never been greater. Our challenge is to help women and men rediscover the joy of marriage, the life-long fulfilment it can offer, especially those who are reluctant to make a long-term commitment.

This brings me to my second point. While some aspects of the 'revolution' in our approach to marriage and the family have been good, is it possible that something good from the past has been lost? I think this is what my friend from Clare was saying in her letter. I note it was a theme considered in the first Céifin Conference entitled, *Are we Forgetting Something?* The letter suggests that part of what is needed is to help people rediscover the good that comes from faith and prayer – she mentioned the Bible in particular.

This coincides with a key proposal of the recent Synod: in making people more familiar with the Word of God, in an informed and formative way, we can act in support of marriage, the family and the good of society itself.

This is because, as it explains in the *Compendium of the Social Doctrine of the Church*, 'The importance and centrality of the family with regard to the person and society is repeatedly underlined by Sacred Scripture' (n. 209). The family is presented from the very opening pages of the Word of God as, 'The primary place of humanisation for the person and society and the cradle of life and love' (n. 209).

The Family Based on Marriage as the Fundamental Unity of Society

The family is the natural community in which human social nature is experienced. It makes a unique and irreplaceable contribution to the good of society. The family unit is born from the stable and committed communion of persons that marriage provides. 'Communion' has to do with the personal relationship between the 'I' and the 'thou'. 'Community', on the other hand, transcends the 'I' and 'thou' and moves towards a 'society' – a 'we'. The family, therefore, as a community of persons, is the first human 'society'. It is at the very heart of the common good.

The common good 'is the sum total of social conditions which allow people, either as groups or as individuals, to reach their fulfilment more fully and more easily' (*Gaudium et Spes,* n. 26).

The *Catechism of the Catholic Church* (*CCC*) explains it in this way:

> The family is the *original cell of social life.* It is the natural society in which husband and wife are called to give themselves in love and in the gift of life. Authority, stability, and a life of relationships within the family constitute the foundations for freedom, security, and fraternity within society. The family is the community in which, from childhood, one can learn moral values, begin to honour God, and make good use of freedom. Family life is an initiation into life in society. (n. 2207)

The *Catechism* goes on to say:

> A man and a woman united in marriage, together with their children, form a family. This institution is prior to any recognition by public authority, which has an obligation to recognise it. It should be considered the normal reference point by which the different forms of family relationship are to be evaluated. (n. 2202).

Marriage and the family, therefore, are of public interest. They are fundamental to the public good and entitled to special consideration and care from the State. Other relationships, whether they are sexual or not, are the result of private interest. They do not have the same fundamental relationship to the good of society and to the bringing up of children as the family based on marriage.

At the heart of this understanding of marriage is a truth taught by Scripture and confirmed by human reason. It is the truth that 'Physical ... *difference* and *complementarity* of a woman and man are oriented toward the goods of marriage and the flourishing of family life' (*CCC*, n. 2333). Being a man or woman is not accidental to who we are or to God's plan for the family and society – it is essential to it.

This is why the Church holds that the good of persons and the proper functioning of society are closely connected with the healthy state of marriage and family life. In the words of the *Compendium of the Social Doctrine of the Church*, 'Without families that are strong in their communion and stable in their commitment,' societies grow weak. This is also why, 'Relegating the family to a subordinate or secondary role, excluding it from its rightful position in society, would be to inflict great harm on the authentic growth of society as a whole.'

The Positive State of Marriage in Irish Life

Some will argue that this presents an idealised view of marriage and family life. They will point out that the concept of a nuclear family of father and mother, united by marriage and bringing up children in a stable and loving environment, does not capture the reality or the ideal of an increasing number of people. They will point to the existence of an increasingly diverse range of family units in Irish society, to an increase in long-term cohabitation, to increasing breakdown in marriage and to the prospect of radically new forms of legally recognised relationships as evidence that the model of family revealed by the Scriptures is increasingly irrelevant.

Family Life Today: The Greatest Revolution?

Yet it is worth asking whether these popular assumptions about the state of marriage as the basis of family life in Ireland are actually true? The fact is that life-long marriage remains the preferred choice of the vast majority of men and women in Ireland. Recent research by the Catholic Marriage Care Service, ACCORD, for example, confirmed that the marriage rate in Ireland has 'actually increased in the past 10 years – suggesting something of a "revival" in marriage relative to the mid and late 1990s when the rate fell to historically low levels.'[1] The survey also found that, 'Marriage is a sufficiently rewarding experience such that 9 out of 10 would recommend it to others'. In contrast to the view that the traditional family unit revealed in the Word of God is no longer relevant, the report concluded, 'The traditional family arrangement of children being raised by both their natural parents is the one preferred by almost all married couples in our survey'.[2]

This is a far cry from any sense of crisis that the family based on marriage is sometimes portrayed in public debate. While some 12 per cent of couples in Ireland chose long-term cohabitation instead of marriage, the family based on marriage is still the fundamental unit of our society by a substantial margin. It continues to play an essential part in the well-being and stability of Irish life. In the words of the ACCORD report in Ireland: 'Healthy, happy marriages [still] make for strong family life; and strong families contribute to the economy and demand little in return from the taxpayer. In other words, "family capital" is at the core of "social capital", upon which we build the future for our country'.[3]

It is this essential link between 'family capital' and 'social capital' that in part explains the special place afforded to marriage in the Irish Constitution. Article 40.1.1 of *Bunreacht na hÉireann* recognises the family 'as the natural primary and fundamental unit group of Society, and as a moral institution possessing inalienable and imprescriptible rights, antecedent and superior to all positive law.'

It is not accurate to suggest that this is merely a remnant of Catholic influence on the formulation of the Constitution, and therefore to be rejected as anachronistic or sectarian. Similar recognition and terminology can be found in the Constitutions of many other countries around the world. The Greek Constitution, for example, describes the family as 'the foundation of the conservation and progress of the nation.' Such values are also consistent with Article 16 of the Universal Declaration of Human Rights, which states: 'The family is the natural and fundamental unit of society and is entitled to protection by society and the State.' Article 16 of the Social Charter of Europe (1961), Article 23 of the International Treaty on Civil Rights, Article 10 of the International Charter on Economic, Social and Cultural Rights, as well as many other national and international instruments, affirm and develop this basic insight that the family is the nucleus of society, and for that reason deserving of special status, development and care.

Proposed Changes to Legislation and Policy

It is on this basis too that Article 41.3.1 of *Bunreacht na hÉireann* places an obligation on the Irish Government to guard the institution of marriage with special care. This brings me to the sensitive and complex issue of the government's stated intention to legislate for a variety of relationships other than marriage, notably for cohabiting and same-sex couples.

In its submission to the Oireachtas All-Party Committee on the Constitution on this issue, the Committee on the Family of the Irish Bishops' Conference in February 2005 acknowledged, and I quote:

> A diversity of family forms support the fundamental human activities of care, intimacy and belongingness to varying degrees, yet it is appropriate that the Constitution should guard with special care the institution of marriage. [However] such a commitment to special care of the family based on marriage ought not, nor does it, prevent the State from seeking to offer appropriate support to individuals in other forms of family units. (p. 6)

The issue, then, is not whether it is appropriate to introduce policies and legislation which provide some level of protection for people in relationships of long-term dependency, in many circumstances this will be totally appropriate and just. The question is at what point such legislation or policy begins to undermine the family based on marriage as the fundamental unit of society and thereby undermine the common good?

In this regard, the publication by government of the *General Scheme of Civil Partnership Bill* in June 2008 gives cause for concern. Obviously, we must await the publication of the actual legislation arising from the scheme to make a complete assessment. It is clear, however, that the General Scheme envisages the possibility that the government will grant to cohabiting and same-sex couples the status of marriage in all but name. Some restrictions will apply to adoption by same-sex couples. Apart from this, however, and given reports from the Department of Justice have confirmed that 'Social welfare and tax entitlements on a par with those of spouses will be provided through the finance and social welfare Bills', it is difficult to see how anything other than the introduction of *de facto* marriage for cohabiting and same-sex couples is envisaged.

Those who are committed to the probity of the Constitution, to the moral integrity of the Word of God and to the precious human value of marriage between a man and a woman as the foundation of society, may have to pursue all avenues of legal and democratic challenge to the published legislation if this is the case.

The intention is not to penalise those who have chosen or find themselves in different family forms or relationships, it is rather to uphold the principle that the family based on marriage between a man and woman is so intimately connected to the good of society that it is deserving of special care and protection. The value of the Constitutional guarantees given in this area cannot be limited to the wording of the Constitution about marriage and the family remaining unchanged. The relevant Articles of the Constitution are more than a statement of aspiration. They imply that the State will maintain a qualitative difference between the level of support and entitlements provided by the State to the family based on marriage and that afforded to other forms of dependent relationship.

This makes the stated intention of government to remove the category 'Marital Status' and to replace it with 'Civil Status' through the Equal Status Act particularly worrying. Some might argue that it is in fact a breach of the government's Constitutional duty to protect the institution of marriage. Those who believe in the values espoused by the Constitution are entitled to ask why such a profound and unnecessary change is envisaged along with others that may yet emerge. Marriage, and with it the common good, is directly undermined when legislation and policy reduce marriage to simply another form of relationship among others.

It is worth noting in this regard that the definition of marriage for the purposes of the Constitution has been judicially interpreted as, 'The voluntary union of one man and one woman to the exclusion of all others for life.'[4]

Family Life Today: The Greatest Revolution?

The Issue of Equality

Some have argued that what is at stake here is the principle of equality. This is to argue that what is being compared are two things which are qualitatively the same. This is manifestly not the case. The link between a public commitment to life-long marriage and the stability of the family unit, as well as the distinct role of a mother and father in the generation and education of children, give marriage a unique and qualitatively different relationship to society than any other form of relationship.

In the words of the Pontifical Council for the Family in 2000:

> Equality before the law must respect the principle of justice which means treating equals equally, and what is different differently: i.e., to give each one his due in justice. This principle of justice would be violated if de facto unions were given a juridical treatment similar or equivalent to the family based on marriage. If the family based on marriage and de facto unions are neither similar nor equivalent in their duties, functions and services in society, then they cannot be similar or equivalent in their juridical status.[5]

This qualitative difference between the family based on marriage and other forms of relationship is increasingly recognised in research. For example, one of the largest surveys on family life to date, the British Millennium Cohort Study (2008), has found that one in four children of cohabiting parents suffer family breakdown before they start school at the age of five, compared to just one in ten children of married parents. Other studies in Britain and the US suggest that children born outside of marriage are more likely to do worse at school, suffer poorer health and are more likely to face problems of unemployment, drugs and crime. In the words of one commentator: 'The strong implication for governments is that they should be doing more to support marriages'.

All the more remarkable, then, is that Ireland looks set to repeat the mistakes of societies like Britain and the US by introducing legislation that will promote cohabitation, remove most incentives to marry and grant same-sex couples the same rights as marriage in all but adoption. This will effectively dissolve the special status of marriage between a man and woman enshrined in the Constitution. This would indeed be a revolution, perhaps the greatest revolution in the history of the Irish family – as the title of the Conference suggests! – but will it be a revolution that promotes the common good of our society? Will it really help children and married couples, or will it further erode marriage at a time when research and experience point to the value of marriage for children and society?

Whether what is envisaged will breach the Constitution remains to be seen, but no one should underestimate how radical and far-reaching the legislation arising from the *General Scheme* published by the government could be. *The priority of the family over society and over the State have to be reaffirmed. The family does not exist for society or the State, but society and the State exist for the family.*

What is being proposed by the government undermines the very principle of equality it claims to uphold. It limits the provision of support in the *General Scheme* to relationships that are presumed to be sexual. This is unjust to those in established relationships of dependency that are not sexual. It confirms that what is driving the change in legislation and policy in this area is not a concern for equality at all. The provision of just, reasonable and much needed support to those in established and dependent relationships that are not sexual in nature has been ignored in the *General Scheme*. Anyone in a caring, dependent relationship, whether sexual or not, should be given certain protections such as hospital visitation rights and a stability of residence in the event of that relationship ending. Why should people in such relationships be discriminated against because their relationship is not sexual? There is need to address important issues of fairness to people in established relationships of dependency. This is possible without undermining the unique role of marriage in society and its contribution to the common good.

More Support for Marriage: A Benefit to Society

Marriage deserves to be supported by society. It is so fundamental to the common good that the State acts in the interests of society when it supports marriage through benefits in taxation, social welfare and social policy.

If we have the good of children and of society at heart, then it is also clear that we need to try to maximise the number of children being raised by a married mother and father. We can do this through providing positive incentives and the formation of positive social attitudes to marriage. We also need to provide greater support for married couples themselves as they live out their life-long commitment to each other and their children. This includes providing more adequate preparation for marriage. ACCORD is involved in outstanding work in this regard, for which they deserve to be applauded. Two of the greatest obstacles ACCORD encounter, however, is the difficulty in acquiring a sufficient number of volunteer counsellors and a general resistance on the part of couples to attend a marriage preparation course. In other countries, for example Italy, the pre-marriage courses consist of at least nine weekend sessions. Here in Ireland it is much less. In spite of this, priests often comment on how couples will spend any amount of time with the florist, the photographer or the hotel manager in preparation for their wedding. These arrangements are important, but the time given to them can be in strong contrast to the willingness of couples to take time out together to reflect on the importance and meaning of what they are about to do.

Conclusion

During my thirteen years on the staff of the Irish College, it was my privilege to marry a great number of couples – hundreds, maybe even thousands. As an aside, I have to say that some of the best people in all those couples came from Clare. I am not saying that because the Céifin Conference is held in Clare, but because I believe it and have believed it for many years. My abiding impression is one of people who had high hopes and earnest dreams for a happy and fulfilling life together. No one I know has ever entered marriage with the expectation or desire that it would fail. The Church offers the compassion of Christ for all those who suffer in this way. It invites all of us to have compassion and to offer practical support for those whose marriages have broken down.

It is here that we come back to our starting point: 'The Word of God in the life and mission of the Church'. Jesus was born and lived in a family, with all its characteristic features. At the wedding feast in Cana he conferred on marriage the highest dignity of a sacrament. Jesus could have produced the wine without the help of the stewards, but he decided to involve them and Mary in the process. I see this as an indication that in God's design the community, particularly the immediate family, have a part to play in supporting marriage. There may be a lot of jokes about prying in-laws, but the extended family have a vital role to play in supporting marriage.

Family Life Today: The Greatest Revolution?

In the story of Cana we also observe how Mary was sensitive to the needs of the newly married couple. Instead of wringing her hands when the wine ran out, an obvious cause of embarrassment and possibly of conflict for the couple, she gets involved, telling the stewards, 'Do whatever he tells you'. In this she points all newly married couples to the true source of their happiness and success in marriage – seeking the will of God in all things together.

It was this that was identified as a particular virtue in the life and marriage of Blessed Louis and Zelie Martin, the parents of the Little Flower, St Thérèse of Lisieux. They were beatified on 19 October 2008 by Pope Benedict. It was Mission Sunday. They are only the second spouses in history to be declared blessed as a couple.

How appropriate, then, that as Ireland prepares to consider legislation with the potential to undermine God's will for marriage and the family, we turn to the example and inspiration of this married couple and draw strength and direction from it. How well we remember the wonderful welcome that was given to the relics of their daughter, St Thérèse of Lisieux, some years ago. The Martin family of nine children and parents who were fully engaged in business, social and Church life, are a timely source of encouragement for all those who promote the value of the family based on marriage in our society.

The Word of God is pro-love, pro-marriage, pro-family, pro-life and pro-society. My prayer is that, through the intercession of Blessed Louis and Zelie Martin, more and more people will rediscover this revolutionary message of the Word of God, for the sake of our society and its future.

Notes

1   *Married Life – The First 7 Years: a survey of married life and couples in the first seven years of marriage in Ireland,* ACCORD Catholic Marriage Care Service, Maynooth, 2007, p. 6.

2   Ibid., p. 38.

3   Ibid.

4   B v R [1995] 1 ILRM 491 per Costello J; it should be noted that the above statement was made prior to the fifteenth amendment to the Constitution, hence the inclusion of the words 'for life'.

5   *Pontifical Council for the Family, Marriage and De Facto Unions,* Holy See, 2000, n. 10.

Family Well-Being

Kieran McKeown
Social and Economic Research Consultant

Introduction

Now that the economy is in recession, it is probably a good time to talk about well-being, because it raises questions about what well-being is anyway, what influences it and what influence might the recession have on it. There are many ways of defining and measuring well-being, and the main purpose of my paper is to offer some insights, based on studies which I have carried out in the past few years with my colleagues, Trutz Haase and Jonathan Pratschke, on the actual experience of well-being and the factors which influence it in different areas and groups within Ireland.

Trends in Well-Being

Well-being has been measured in Ireland since 1973 using a very simple question: 'All things considered, how satisfied are you with your life as a whole these days?' This is the question used by Eurobarometer (since 1973) as well as by the European Values Study (in 1980, 1990 and 2000), and by the European Foundation (in 2003).[1] We can judge from these surveys how Ireland fares relative to other EU countries, and also judge how the Celtic Tiger impacted on Irish well-being.

From these studies, we know that Ireland, including Northern Ireland, is among the group of countries that scores consistently high in terms of life satisfaction. On a four-point scale, Ireland tends to score about 3.2, while on a ten-point scale, Ireland's score is around 8.0. What is particularly interesting is that there has been no substantial improvement in life satisfaction since the onset of the economic boom in 1994. This is because Ireland's well-being scores are already close to the upper limit of the scale, giving rise to what Tony Fahey has called the 'ceiling effect'.[2] This suggests that, above a certain level of income, economic growth does not generate increasing levels of well-being, although economic growth may be needed to sustain existing levels of well-being as expectations continue to rise.

Of course, averages can be deceptive and some groups in Ireland are below the mean of 8.2 – such as the those who are unemployed (mean score of 7.18 in the European Values Study) and those who are separated/divorced (mean score of 7.32 in the European Values Study) – but these are still in the upper half of the scale and well above the mean scores for poorer countries such as Greece (6.7) and Belarus (4.8).[3]

The last recession in Ireland was over twenty years ago, in 1986/7, and life satisfaction scores for the country dipped below 3.0. However, by 1990 they were fully recovered, even before the Celtic Tiger came about, and they have remained unchanged at that level.

A Broader Understanding of Well-Being

These findings are interesting and informative and may help to allay some of the anxieties about the present recession by putting it in a broader perspective, and by underlining the relatively weak link between well-being and economic growth. However, these findings are based on a rather narrow concept of well-being, and are of fairly limited value from the perspective of understanding how one might improve well-being. Most of the research that we have done on well-being has been commissioned by organisations like Respond! Housing Association, Barnardos and local development organisations like Partnership Companies. All of these have a particular commitment to helping people who have difficulty coping with life's adversities, such as accessing housing, bringing up children in poverty, living in difficult and even dangerous neighbourhoods, and so on. Our approach to the issue of well-being, therefore, is to apply the skills of research to measure well-being as accurately and as comprehensively as possible, and to analyse the factors that influence it so that these organisations can intervene effectively to promote the well-being of the people they serve.

It is true that well-being includes life satisfaction, as measured in Eurobarometer and other surveys. However, life itself has many other domains including the thoughts, feelings and hopes about oneself and one's abilities, the family relationships with one's partner and one's children, and the broader social environment where one lives, including one's support networks, the quality of neighbourhood and access to services. Over the past few years, we have collected data on all these domains using the most scientific instruments available. In fact, this work grew out of a study commissioned in 2003 by the Céifin Centre and the Family Support Agency – on family well-being – and that is why I am particularly happy to 'report back' to Céifin, as it were, on the progress we have made since that study.

For the purpose of this paper, we have combined four different studies of well-being, involving 1,212 interviews in different parts of the country (notably Limerick City, Bray, County Wicklow, and residents in Respond! housing estates). Each study used the same set of validated instruments to measure different aspects of well-being, and that is why it is possible to combine them into a single dataset and to use statistical analysis – specifically structural equation modelling – to assess how the experiences of these respondents can throw light on the nature of well-being.

Before reporting the actual results, it might be useful to make two points. First, we take well-being as our starting point and explore the diverse ways in which this is manifested. This seems preferable to taking the family as our starting point and exploring the factors which influence its well-being. The rationale for this approach is that it allows the determinants of family well-being to be explored in the context of other forms of well-being, thereby underlining their commonality. Naturally, this is not the only approach possible, and it underlines the importance of one's starting point, since how one thinks about the family will also tend to influence the type of analysis and the type of results. Second, although each sample was randomly selected, the combined sample is not necessarily representative of the Irish population. Its value, however, lies not in its representativeness, but in the robustness of the model in explaining the connection between the different aspects of well-being and their underlying causes.

The overall model of well-being which emerges from these studies is summarised in Figure 1 at the end of this chapter. The results indicate that overall well-being is a subjective state with three key dimensions. The first is personal well-being and is measured by life satisfaction, depression and hope (sometimes called locus of control). The second is relational well-being and is measured by the relationship with one's partner, one's child and the parent's perception of the child's difficulties. The third is environmental well-being and is measured by the availability of social supports, the existence of local problems in the neighbourhood (such as its appearance, safety, noise and litter) and access to local services (such as playgrounds, parks, sports facilities, schools, public transport and shops). What is significant about this model is that overall well-being explains about three-quarters of the variance in well-being within the combined sample. In statistical terms, this is a very powerful result and unusual in that so much variability is explained by a relatively simple model.

Factors Influencing Well-Being

We also analysed some of the more important factors which influence overall well-being, which shows that most of the variation in well-being – more than two-thirds – is explained by just three variables:

- Positive affect (the frequency of experiencing emotions such as feeling enthusiastic, strong, interested, alert active and inspired);
- Negative affect (the frequency of experiencing emotions such as feeling distressed, upset, afraid);
- Socio-economic status (which includes age completed full-time education, in paid work, home ownership, Medical Card and financial stress).

By the usual standards of statistical analysis, this is a strong and significant result, and provides an important roadmap not only for understanding well-being, but also for informing strategies to support those whose well-being is weak or vulnerable. That is why it is important to spend some time now in teasing out the implications of these results.

Implications of Broader Understanding of Well-being

The results that I have just outlined are in line with what most people might describe as 'common sense'. However, it is important to emphasise that this common sense approach is supported by the evidence, based on detailed interviews with

1,212 people on their experience of well-being. The lessons that I now draw from this analysis are strongly influenced by the purposes for which the data was collected, which is to assist organisations like Respond!, Barnardos and local development groups like Partnership Companies to address the needs of people whose well-being is vulnerable. For this reason, these lessons may be particularly relevant to those who work with vulnerable individuals, families and communities.

First, in view of the importance of positive and negative emotions, it is important to be clear what these concepts entail. These are two independent aspects of the personality, not polar opposites; each person has elements of both and can be simultaneously strong or weak on both. Positive emotions are typically associated with an action-orientation geared towards pleasure and reward, and is regarded by psychologists as adaptive to procuring resources for survival.[4] Negative emotions are typically associated with a withdrawal-orientation, geared towards avoiding pain and other undesirable consequences. It is also regarded by psychologists as adaptive for survival by keeping out of danger. Positive emotions are also related to extraversion and sociability, as well as to cheerfulness, enthusiasm and energy; while negative emotions are related to fear/anxiety, sadness/depression and anger/hostility. Both these dimensions mirror optimism and pessimism and, whether one is a 'strategic optimist' or a 'defensive pessimist', both have a role to play in personality, and both have their strengths and limitations.[5] However, in view of our finding that positive emotions have a positive influence on overall well-being, and negative emotions have a negative influence, it is worth emphasising the importance of cultivating positive emotions. The good news about positive emotions is that they are not very dependent upon external circumstances, as a leading researcher in this field has observed: 'People do not require all that much – in terms of material conditions, life circumstances, and so on – to feel cheerful, enthusiastic, and interested in life. Thus, one need not be young or wealthy or have a glamorous, high-paying job in order to be happy. This, in turn, suggests that virtually anyone is capable of experiencing substantial levels of positive affectivity'.[6] This, in turn, is consistent with our finding that positive affect is a more significant influence on overall well-being compared to economic resources.

Second, our analysis indicates that a person's psychological resources (specifically their habitual ways of thinking and feeling) and their economic resources (specifically their income and entitlements) combine to influence overall well-being. In other words, a person's well-being is shaped by their 'internal environment' (comprising thoughts and feelings) and their 'external environment' (comprising economic resources). Our study did not cover one-off adverse events such as an accident or illness, a sudden loss of income or wealth, or the break-up of an intimate relationship, although these are also likely to show an adverse effect on well-being. However, it is significant that the diverse forms of well-being in the model can be traced back to just two core determinants: psychological resources and economic resources.

Third, it is noteworthy that a person's psychological resources – specifically their habitual ways of thinking and feeling – have a greater influence on well-being than the amount of their economic resources. This is worth noting, not because it is a new finding,[7] but because public debate on well-being often tends to focus excessively, if not exclusively, on economic resources. This analysis suggests the need to recognise the importance of psychological resources in shaping well-being because of their crucial role in strengthening resilience to adversity. By the same reasoning, our analysis also called attention to the limits of economic resources in promoting well-being, a finding that has already been confirmed by the experience of the Celtic Tiger.

Fourth, the results indicate that psychological resources and economic resources are in fact interconnected. This arises because we know that a positive attitude helps to increase economic resources such as productivity and opportunities for promotion, while economic resources in turn improve positive affect by creating opportunities for enjoyment.[8] Similarly, negative affect can reduce economic resources by making a person less employable, while the experience of financial hardship can also induce and reinforce negative feelings.

Fifth, it is well-recognised that a person's psychological resources are the outcome of both genetic and environmental factors, and this has given rise to the concept of a happiness 'set point' or 'set range'. In the past, there was a tendency to frame this issue in terms of 'nature versus nurture', but researchers now recognise that nature interacts with nurture in a wide range of circumstances to produce very different outcomes, due to the human capacity for adaptation. One recent review of this issue concluded: 'The happiness set point is not really a set point at all, but a "set range". Although there are genetic influences on our happiness ... change is possible for all people.'[9] Given that every personality trait has a genetic, and therefore heritable, dimension, the interesting research question is: why are some traits more changeable than others?[10] However, even when habitual patterns of thought and feeling seem resistant to change, this knowledge can itself be of considerable benefit to people with, for example, depressive symptoms, by virtue of acknowledging that this personality trait is a natural tendency, which is not 'wrong' or a 'mistake'. This awareness can assist the person in learning to live with this trait, while recognising its dangers and limitations. Interventions which promote this form of self-knowledge could have the effect of relieving symptoms of depression by helping the person find constructive ways of living with their natural tendencies.

Sixth, the model provides a simple roadmap to suggest that people who need help typically require either some psychological assistance in order to think and feel differently about their problems, or some practical assistance to overcome their economic resource difficulties – maybe even both. As with any roadmap, it is first necessary to establish where you are on the map. This means that the map can also act as a diagnostic tool to help identify the areas where difficulties are being experienced, which may be in any one of the nine domains: life satisfaction, depression, hope, relationship with partner, relationship with children, children's difficulties, support network, local problems and local services. Given the inter-dependent nature of well-being, intervention in any one domain is likely to have spill-over effects in all of the other domains. However, in all domains, the predominant focus will be on building the person's psychological and economic resources as appropriate.

Seventh, the finding that positive affect is the single most important influence on well-being does not imply a simplistic 'be positive' approach to problems. Being positive does not exclude the negative, or exclude pretending that life is better because of adversity. Rather, it seeks to achieve a balance where positive thoughts and feelings outweigh the negative. The insights of cognitive psychology[11] and positive psychology[12] are directly relevant in this context. A key insight of cognitive therapy is that a person's psychological and emotional well-being can be increased by changing the way they think about the past, the present and the future.[13] For example, feelings about the past can be changed by questioning the ideology that the past determines the present, and by cultivating forgiveness and gratitude towards past events. Feelings about the present can be changed through activities such as socialising and physical exercise and absorption in other meaningful endeavours, savouring the moment and living mindfully; while positive feelings about the future can be increased through hope and optimism. This is consistent with the 'broaden-and-build theory of positive emotions',[14] which suggests that people with more positive emotions tend to have a greater capacity for building friendships and support networks, as well as being more creative at solving problems and challenges in everyday life.[15] In other words, people with more positive emotions are more likely to see the world in terms of expansionary 'win-win' options, rather than contractionary 'win-lose' options. In addition, cultivating positive emotions has been shown to encourage those qualities, such as persistence, flexibility and resourcefulness, which are essential to solving problems.[16] In line with this, the authors of a recent book on happiness research recommend the 'AIM' model of positive thinking, where AIM is an acronym denoting attention (such as looking for the positives in the self, others and events), interpretation (such as framing things with optimism, appreciation and gratitude) and memory (such as reminiscing on good times, recalling past successes and cultivating forgiveness).[17]

Eighth, while the results of our analysis highlight the two key elements in any strategy to promote well-being – namely enhancing psychological and economic resources – the precise tactics will depend on a more detailed assessment of the severity of the condition, the motivation to change, the preferences of the person(s) seeking help, what is known to work, what resources are available, and other circumstances. These tactics may involve individual work, group work, family work, community work – or combinations of each – but all focused on the same strategy. It is also worth remembering that the well-being of individuals, their families and their communities is systematically interconnected. Well-being flows freely between the porous boundaries of the personal, the relational and the community. The linkages within the model are presented in linear form and, while this is accurate in its own right, a more complete understanding would represent these linkages as part of a circular or even spiral pattern of cause and effect. This would underline how intervention at any point in the system is likely to have a ripple effect, as the process of cause and effect unfolds over time. Any intervention should also take account of the fact that measures to improve the well-being of children are most likely to be effective when they also improve the well-being of parents.

Ninth, it has been recognised for some time that national accounts of well-being, parallel to economic accounts, would help to reflect the importance of well-being for individuals, families, communities and society in general. The model I have outlined highlights some of the domains where measurements might be undertaken with a view to tracking changes in well-being generally, and identifying individuals and groups who may be vulnerable to falling below acceptable thresholds of well-being. The maxim that 'what gets measured gets valued' applies to well-being also, and the implementation of a system for national accounts of well-being would help society to focus more explicitly on improving well-being and bring greater refinement in understanding how well-being can be promoted in different settings.

Tenth, and finally, it is important to state that well-being, as the term suggests, is a quality of being itself; to be is to be well. Well-being is experienced because it already exists, not because it is created anew. Indeed, it could not be experienced unless it already existed, and would not be sought unless we already knew it to be part of our nature. In the same way as educators speak of intelligence as being revealed through the process of learning and unlearning, so well-being is manifested by removing obstacles that block one from experiencing it. This perspective is important because it underlines how well-being is like the sun; we know it never ceases to shine even though we speak of it as rising and setting, and of shining only when the sky is cloudless. Similarly, well-being always shines but other thoughts and feelings can cloud it over. This is the metaphysical foundation of positive thinking because it allows life's adversities to be framed as passing difficulties rather than permanent deficits, and to recognise that since well-being is the condition which sustains life itself, everyone is already well, but just not fully aware of it.

Notes

1   Eurobarometer measures the responses on a four-point scale from 'not satisfied at all' (1) to 'very satisfied' (4), whereas European Values Study and the European Foundation Study use a ten-point scale from dissatisfied (1) to satisfied (10). Results of Eurobarometer and European Values Study are analysed in Fahey, T., 'How do we feel? Economic boom and happiness', in T. Fahey, H. Russell and C.T. Whelan (eds), *Best of Times? The Social Impact of the Celtic Tiger*, Dublin: Institute of Public Administration, 2007, pp.11–26; and Fahey, T., Hayes, B. and Sinnott, R., *Conflict and Consensus: A Study of Values and attitudes in the Republic of Ireland and Northern Ireland*, Dublin: Institute of Public Administration, 2005, pp.162–184. Results of the European Foundation Study are reported in Bohnke, P., *First European Quality of Life Survey: Life Satisfaction, Happiness and Sense of Belonging*, Dublin: European Foundation for the Improvement of Living and Working Conditions, 2003.

2   Fahey, T., 'How do we feel? Economic boom and happiness' in T. Fahey, H. Russell and C.T. Whelan (eds), *Best of Times? The Social Impact of the Celtic Tiger*, Dublin: Institute of Public Administration, 2007, pp.11–26.

3   Fahey, T., Hayes, B. and Sinnott, R., *Conflict and Consensus: A Study of Values and Attitudes in the Republic of Ireland and Northern Ireland*, Dublin: Institute of Public Administration, 2005, pp.162–184.

4   See Watson, D., 'Positive Affectivity: The Disposition to Experience Pleasurable Emotional States', in C.R. Snyder and S. Lopez (eds), *Handbook of Positive Psychology*, New York: Oxford University Press, 2002.

5   See Norem, J.K., *The Positive Power of Negative Thinking: Using Defensive Pessimism to Harness Anxiety and Perform at Your Peak*, Cambridge, MA: Basic Books, 2001.

6   Watson, D., 2002, 'Positive Affectivity: The Disposition to Experience Pleasurable Emotional States', in C.R. Snyder and S. Lopez (eds), *Handbook of Positive Psychology*, New York: Oxford University Press, p.115.

7   A similar conclusion emerged from a recent review of the literature on child outcomes, which observed that socio-economic indicators 'have relatively limited utility as guides for designing effective interventions because they tell us relatively little about the causal mechanisms that explain their impacts on child development. Thus, researchers and service providers are focusing increasingly on the importance of within-group variability and individual differences among children and families.' Shonkoff, J.P. and D.A. Phillips, (eds), *Neurons to Neighbourhoods: The Science of Early Childhood Development*, Washington DC: National Academy Press, 2000, p. 354.

8   Diener, E. and Biswas-Diner, R., *Happiness: Unlocking the Mysteries of Psychological Wealth*, Oxford UK: Blackwell Publishing, 2008, pp.68–85.

9   Ibid., p. 162.

10   Seligman, M., *Authentic Happiness: Using the New Positive Psychology to Realise your Potential for Lasting Fulfilment*, New York: The Free Press, 2002, p. 47.

11   See, for example, www.beckinstitute.org.

12   Seligman, M., *Authentic Happiness: Using the New Positive Psychology to Realise your Potential for Lasting Fulfilment*, New York: The Free Press, 2002.

13   See, for example, Snyder, CR. and Lopez, S. (eds)*, Handbook of Positive Psychology*, pp. 120–134, New York: Oxford University Press, 2002; see also www.beckinstitute.org.

14   Fredrickson, B., 'Positive Emotions', in ibid., pp. 120–134.

15   Carr, A., *Positive Psychology: The Science of Happiness and Human Strengths*, Hove and New York: Brunner-Routledge, 2004, pp. 13–15.

16   For more information, visit the Positive Psychology Center at www.positivepsychology.org.

17   Diener, E. and Biswas-Diner, R., *Happiness: Unlocking the Mysteries of Psychological Wealth*, Oxford, UK: Blackwell Publishing, 2008, Chapter 11.

Figure 1: Model of Well-Being

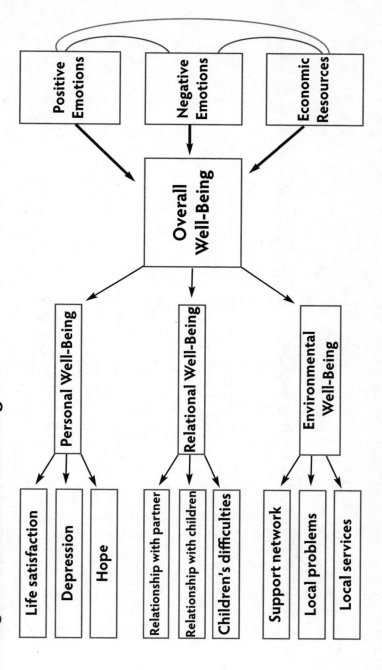

Home and Work

Nomads – Will They Change the Family?

Charles Handy
Writer, Broadcaster and Lecturer

(This paper was written in conjunction with a series of family photographs taken by Elizabeth Handy, which can be found at page 65.)

Introduction

Work has always structured the way that we live. If you think back to the agricultural economy, which still existed in parts of Ireland in my youth, everything happened around the home and everybody stayed at home, in a sense. When I grew up in Kildare, everybody that I knew had their midday meal at home. However, then came the industrial revolution, and work moved away from the home and people went *out* to work. Offices replaced factories and the assumption was that you had to have all the people in the same place at the same time to get the work done. You had to move from the home to work, and that actually took the work out of the home.

My rather bumptious teenage daughter once said – I think she was teasing me – 'Until I was twelve, I thought you were the man who came to lunch on Sundays'. To some extent, she was right. I used to leave before the kids woke up and I was back after they were in bed again, so they only saw me at weekends and in the holidays. As a result, they had no idea what I did for work in the sense of earning money. After all, the only adults you meet when you're a child are parents and teachers, so you have a very strange idea of what work is.

I remember when my seven-year-old son came back from school one day and said they had been asked to write an essay on what their father does. 'Oh,' I said, 'that's very interesting.

What did you say I did?' I wondered how he described my life as a business professor. 'I said you were a painter.' 'Oh!' – maybe he had discovered some hidden talent in me – 'What did you say I paint?' 'Oh, walls', he said. The only time he had seen me actually doing anything constructive in the home was painting the walls of the house! Therefore, he had no idea what work outside the home really meant.

Nowadays, more people spend at least part of their time in what is called the knowledge economy or the information age: processing data, information, images, and so on – this can be done anywhere. We are nomads, Bedouins; we carry our work with us. You can work anywhere you like: on an airplane, on the train, on a bus, or at home. Increasingly, people spend one or more days working from home if their bosses allow it, and their bosses would do well to allow it, because corralling employees, bringing them into the place of work, is incredibly expensive. Buildings cost money and, if you think about it, buildings are empty for two-thirds of the time. Therefore, the more people you can push out of the building to somewhere else and bring them in only for necessary meetings and so on, the cheaper it will be – and in my view the more liberating it will be. Of course you have to trust people to work when they're out of your sight, and that's not that easy. What I am interested in is the effect it has on the family once you bring people back into the home.

Most children now have some image of what work really means, as they see one or other of their parents working. The home is the really important classroom in life. Schools teach you useful things but it is in the home you learn the important things. That's where you learn self-discipline, consideration for others, the limits to decent behaviour and you learn what's right and what's wrong. Of course, you could also learn horrible lessons if you belong to a bad family, like that it is okay to beat your wife, for example. But in a good family you learn the really important things in life and one of the these is work: the discipline of work, the accountability of work, the responsibility of work. How else do you learn about it unless you see somebody doing it? In this funny schoolroom that is the family, you don't have people preaching to you or teaching you or lecturing you most of the time. You learn by watching; it is a sort of unconscious, subliminal schoolroom. I wish to goodness that when we were young parents we had known that. We were so busy with our own lives that we didn't even think about it, but of course the way we behaved was going to be imitated and copied by our children. Little did we realise that when we shouted at each other they would think that was acceptable behaviour, but now I wish we had been wiser in our youth. Families are the important schoolroom of life.

Photograph One – The Handys' House
Our present home is a garden apartment. The house was a family house when it was built in 1890. The family in those days included at least three generations, plus all the people who worked with and for the family. Now that house is divided into seven apartments, but the same number of people live in it now as one hundred and twenty years ago. We have tried to bring back some of that old idea of a family as all-embracing, in that our two children with their families live in two other apartments of the house, but they have their own front doors. So, we are separate yet together, which I believe is the essence of a good family. We are individual, but bonded together in some way. The danger in society is that families are getting pushed into smaller and smaller units, so that the idea of all being together in one place and at one time as a family is rare now. Here lies the problem – how can you be bonded together as well as being separate?

My wife Elizabeth and I thought that it would be important to see how families are actually coping these days with this new kind of nomadic workforce, in other words, people who occasionally pop into the office and actually work at home. It so happened that we were asked to prepare a photographic image on 'the family' for another conference that was taking place in London. We decided to photograph three families – but how does one photograph a family?

First Family

Photograph Two – The Surrey Family
This is the first of the three families. I can tell you that it's a family with seven children, of whom only four were present because three of them are grown-up, living abroad and working. It's a decent Catholic family with seven children, but that doesn't tell you very much, except that they live in a reasonably respectable suburban house. The husband is a psychiatrist who works mostly in a hospital but occasionally at home. The wife was a part-time teacher but is now an art student. However, the parents' professions don't tell you very much about how they live or what kind of family they are, so Elizabeth decided to look at how they actually do their work in the home. You will notice that this is a slightly 'jumbled up' picture to convey this image of the individual being together with the family – and of course they're happy because they're photographed individually and not always as a group.

Photograph Three – The Surrey Family at Work
This is the family at work, and you may notice that they are beginning to pick up habits from the father and others; this is his workplace, which is his study. Another aspect of a family, a good family, is that they are actually looking after each other and caring.

Nomads – Will They Change the Family?

Photograph Four –The Surrey Family Caring
Here you see them actually in the kitchen/dining room, in one way or another taking care of the family and helping out. The father is invigilating his daughter on the catechism, just to show what a decently religious family they are.

Photograph Five – The Surrey Family Sharing
This is the family together, actually sharing in a family decision. In this case, they were planning an extension to the house. The home is an actual classroom, though nobody is really aware of it; the children are learning how to cook, how to lay the table and learning that they have a part in decisions of the family.

Second Family

Photograph Six – The Norfolk Family
Here is another family. This one lives in the country in Norfolk, and the situation is slightly different because, in this case, the wife is the breadwinner. She is an architect who mostly works in the local town, but also partly at home. The husband is the carer in the family. This is a country cottage, so there isn't too much space.

Photograph Seven – The Norfolk Family at Work
You can see the husband in the background – in addition to looking after the family he does some calculations on energy and heating for architects in the houses they design, which he works on at home in his study. It is a very cramped space, as you can see, and if his daughter wants to do her homework in there she has to squat on the step behind her. The wife, Sarah, when she works from home, has to use the kitchen table, because she's the person who is least important in the workplace at home. On the other hand, there is some advantage to this open plan arrangement, compressed and

uncomfortable though it is. It means that at least the children are very aware of work, and the responsibility and preparation that goes along with it.

Photographs Eight and Nine – The Norfolk Family Caring and Sharing
This photograph shows the family caring. The mother-in-law is in this picture. It shows Brad, the husband, looking after the two little children, and they are sharing in the conviviality of being a family, bringing in the neighbours and bringing in the mother-in-law. The extended family these days includes a few other people, and again this is how one learns about relationships and that there is a responsibility due to another generation and indeed to friends.

Third Family

Photograph Ten – The London Family
The London family is our third family and it is a single-parent family. One out of four children in Britain today live in a single-parent family, so this is quite a common thing. Another aspect of the family concerns the eldest daughter, who has a different father. Therefore, like many families these days, you have step-children and step-parents. The London family is a single-parent family because the mother 'chucked him out'. He physically abused her in front of the children, having in his youth seen his father physically abuse his mother. She said, 'I've got to break the cycle, so he had to go; he's not allowed in the house, but the children see him'. Unfortunately, this is a rather typical state of affairs for a lot of families today.

Photograph Eleven – The London Family at Work
Despite this undesirable past, this is a brilliant family, because Fiona, the mother, is a wonderful parent. This photograph shows the family at work; they all have their allocated little

tasks to do, all pinned up on the board. It is a jumble, but again they are seeing what work involves.

Photograph Twelve – The London Family Caring
This is where they're caring for each other. The youngest are bathing; the eldest daughter helps with the laundry. They are all involved in this family.

Photograph Thirteen – The London Family Sharing
This photograph shows all of them having enjoyment and fun in their own way, being separate yet together. I believe that is the secret of a successful family. When you go into this home with all the difficulties, the lack of money and so on, you find it is an incredibly happy place. The children are learning, developing and growing, so I do believe that no matter how difficult a family is, in a sense, it can work if you work at it. I do know there are many families who do not work well; this family is obviously one who are willing to be photographed, so they are quite proud of what they do. They seem to me to be a sign that anybody can make it happen.

The Handy Family

After many years of trying to practise what we preach, eventually in our later years, we decided that we could actually develop a proper kind of space for the family.

Photograph Fourteen –Liz's Different Roles
This is the family room that we created in London before we moved into our garden apartment, when we had a slightly bigger house. This is Elizabeth in our family room/kitchen, where everything happened. This is to show that Elizabeth has three work roles in her life:

- You can see Elizabeth as a photographer, and because she stands nearest to the camera as a photographer, this is her chosen form of work. This is what she really likes doing.
- She is also a homemaker, standing at the stove.
- Right at the back, she is managing our little business and being my agent. You can see how relatively unimportant I am in her life, since that's the smallest of the images!

These are the three work roles that Elizabeth has, pictured in what became our family's space, where it was very clear to our children exactly what work meant in its different forms, because it was happening all around them all the time. It took a long time in our life before we could reach this stage.

My father was a Protestant parson in Kildare in the countryside and he had a study where he spent an awful lot of his time. Though I rejected much of what my parents did, as one does when one is young, in the end I always hankered after a study of my own. I didn't get one until much, much later in my life, when I was in my sixties, and it became a rather grand study.

Photograph Fifteen – Charles' Role

This photograph shows me in my study in the country. If you want a room of your own in which to work, this is the ideal kind of place to have. We are very lucky, but we have been working at it for a long time, because we do believe that having the place right, if you can possibly manage it, is absolutely crucial. Then the family will learn from all of that. It is no accident that our children, now that they are grown up – growing old in a sense, in their late thirties and early forties – have both married people whom they work with from home. Nobody told them to do this, but obviously, as they watched us, they thought that was the way it should be, so they are nomads based in the home. Our son is an actor, so sometimes he is at home too much! Our daughter has married an osteopath. They are both osteopaths and they actually have a treatment room in the house. It is a very bonding kind of marriage. If you work together, live together, eat together and sleep together, it works amazingly well for some people.

As we thought about the family, something struck me. I have spent most of my life looking at organisations of one sort or another, and every organisation that I meet has a purpose or a goal, even if they don't quite specify it properly as a vision. And then you come to a family. Families don't really have goals or purposes, at least not declared ones, so what kind of organisation is it and should it have a purpose or a goal? I think probably not. To bond it together it has to have some kind of shared values or principles, doesn't it?

Still Life

Elizabeth is a very creative photographer, so one of the techniques she has developed is what is called a still life photograph. The old still lifes of the Dutch paintings in the sixteenth and seventeenth centuries showed all the objects that indicated your status in life. Elizabeth has adapted this concept to show the objects that are most *important* in your life. Five objects and one piece of nature – put them on the table and photograph them and this will be your coat of arms, which will describe you.

Photograph Sixteen – Charles' Still Life
This photograph is my still life. On the left-hand side is a camera lens, and that represents my photographer wife. But it's a lens, not a camera, because a lens is a focusing device and so she is not only the woman that I've loved for forty-eight years, she also focuses my life in a very interesting way. The elephant with the flea on top of it is the title of one of my books, *The Elephant and the Flea,* and that signifies my work. In the centre

there is a white stone that I keep on my desk because, some years ago writing a book, I came across a verse in the Book of Revelations, a really strange book: "'To the one who prevails" said the angels "I give a white stone, on which will be written a name, a name that will be known only to the one who receives it.'" I'm not quite sure what it means, but I interpret it as that if I prevail, in other words, if I live up to my possibilities in life, I will deserve my name and so the white stone is there to say, 'live up to your possibilities'.

This lead us to think that it would be interesting if we got a family to compose a still life: to actually sit down together and say what defines us as a family, what pulls us together, what holds us together. I know we're all individuals, but there is this bond that creates us. It is a fantastically interesting exercise.

Photograph Seventeen – The Verity Family Still Life
The Verity family are a young family in London. The centrepiece is an old Italian coffee pot, because, basically, sitting around a table is what holds them together. I'm sure a lot of families do this, but there are homes in London where there are no tables, because they never sit together. Instead, the family members help themselves from the refrigerator and sit in front of the television and eat off their knees. In some cases, in quite wealthy households, each child has a television and a microwave in their bedroom and that is where they go – there is no need for a table. Therefore, the coffeepot is pretty symbolic in this house. Books also play a large part and there is a statue of a mother and two children, the first piece of artwork they bought, which is very symbolic about families.

Photograph Eighteen – The Aston Family
This photograph shows another family and another of Elizabeth's composite photographs, or 'joiners' as she calls them. Here she has tried to show each member of the family as an

individual, doing their own thing in different parts of the room, but also being a family. An old uncle is putting his nose in at the back. The extended family is here, and in the middle of the image is their still life on the table, which they composed.

Photograph Nineteen – The Pearl Family
Lastly, the Pearl family at breakfast in North London. You can see all of those images of the future in those little children. What are they learning? What are they going to draw away from this interesting schoolroom on a Sunday morning in North London?

I leave you with the thought that the way the world is changing is actually bringing families back together again in a funny way, because work is coming home again into the family. Technology can bond people together, even if they aren't able to put their children in the same kind of building. Instead of meeting their children in the garden, they can actually meet them in cyberspace. I know so many grandparents, particularly grandmothers, who spend their time communicating with their grandchildren all around the world through email and Skype. Technology in a strange way is allowing people to be individual but together. Of course, it helps enormously if you can actually join physically together whenever possible around the table or a coffee pot, or better still, a bottle of red wine.

Charles Handy in Conversation with John Quinn

JQ   Thank you Charles, as usual you have energised us and made us think, and given us what Kieran McKeown might describe as some positive emotions.

I half suspect that, when the title came up, *Family Life Today: The Greatest Revolution?*, people may have been thinking dark thoughts about the end of families as we know them, and the death of the family. But there is, of course, another sense or literal meaning of the word revolution – revolving; it is coming back around to perhaps what it had been before. I wonder though about the photographs, are they perhaps a little bit too rosy, too cosy?

CH   In a sense that is correct; obviously if you are going to be photographed as a family you don't show us the warts, you show us the good things. We found if they weren't quite pleased with what they were doing as a family they wouldn't even let us into their homes. The families in the photos weren't dysfunctional families, they were ordinary families. Maybe they are a bit of an ideal, but they wouldn't put themselves forward with that view. They just thought, this is how we live and we would like to show that to the people. Why, I often wonder, do we want to concentrate on the bad and not on the good?

JQ   You did say that there are families who would not work as good schoolrooms or perhaps not be schoolrooms at all. Is there a role there for the State or the employer or society to nourish families like that?

CH These families need an awful lot of help, but I think it would also benefit them to know just what a family could be, because they are probably struggling so much that they can't raise their eyes above the parapet. I'm not sure if the State can help an awful lot. I'm impressed by some charities that do help, like Homestart in Britain, where people move in to help such families in a practical way. Whatever else we do, we are all members of a family at some stage in our lives and we sometimes don't acknowledge the importance of that. We just take it as something that happens in life, but I think it is incredibly important that we build up the family.

JQ When you talk about the growing number of people who are working at least some of the time from home, and the businesses with people who don't have to go into the office – more people using what you call this 'portfolio' life – are they not still a minority? It makes me think of the hordes of commuters travelling into Limerick or Ennis or Dublin. For a lot of people, much as they might like it, there is very little time for family life.

CH That has got to change. I think employers have to understand that this is a crazy way to run a business – to work people so hard that they're so tired they can't actually be at home with their families. It's uneconomic to bring people into work every day and give them a private little apartment of their own, which they can fill with portraits and so on. More and more organisations are turning themselves into what I call clubs, where there are spaces for meetings and particular activities but most people don't have a private place, or even a private desk, because they want to make the maximum use of the space. They talk to each other on the telephone or mostly by email from one floor of the building to the next, when they could perfectly well do that from somewhere else. I believe it will change. At the moment, architects tell me whenever they have to present a house to a developer, the house has to have a study in it, or a study/bedroom, otherwise it won't sell. So the world is moving the way I think it actually should move. However, at the moment, some people actually like leaving home as early as possible and getting back as late as possible, as I did – but they will be known as the man who came to lunch on Sundays! It won't do any good.

JQ   All of this will equally have implications for the future design and architecture not only of offices, but of homes. We are still building houses as they were built a hundred years ago: with a sitting room, a dining room, three bedrooms etc. This has implications for more communal space, private space and office space.

CH   I think so. To buy a house with the 'function', as it were, put over the door of each room so it is labelled a dining room, a sleeping room or a cooking room, is to me much too imprisoning. Elizabeth likes to point out that in our original London home, in the bottom of that big house, we had the kitchen in seven different places over the twenty-five years we lived there. This was because as the family changed and we needed a smaller kitchen or a bigger kitchen or more space for this or less space for particular things. Eventually, we had just one big kitchen where everything happened. I think that homes should be much more versatile and architects should understand this. At the moment, everybody moves house every eight years in England on average. You shouldn't need to do that, you should be able to adapt the house; it would save an awful lot of money. Architects have to pay much more attention to the way the family is going to evolve. I think we will increasingly have to go back to having the other generations with us, to having four-generation families living in the same building, because the cost of putting your aged grandparents into homes is going to be so expensive to society that we might have to behave like decent families and give them a room in our own homes. We don't have space for that at the moment so we will have to adjust.

JQ   You suggested people read Chapter 15 of your book, *Myself and Other More Important Matters*. I suggest they also read, perhaps more importantly, Chapter 14, which is called 'Kennels for Kids'. Can you explain this title?

CH   A Dutch friend of mine said, 'Isn't it very odd that you English keep your dogs at home but you park your kids elsewhere, either in crèches or in boarding schools if you're rich. What a funny way round it is. In Holland we park our dogs in kennels and we keep the kids at home'. I think we should be very careful about delegating the care of our children to other people. Delegate many things in your life, but not your children, in my view.

JQ   Statistics show that 15–20 per cent of a child's time is taken up by school, which raises the question: what about the other 80–85 per cent of the time?

CH   A lot of learning goes on in childhood, but very little of it happens in schools in my view. It happens in the streets and it happens at home — and at least we can sort of control what happens in the home. We can't always control what happens in the streets, but that's where children learn the very important lessons in life about relationships and about standards. Unfortunately, many of the lessons that they learn in the streets are not the ones you might want them to learn, but at least we can do something about the kind of learning that goes on at home, even if it is a very difficult home to run.

JQ   You make the point in your book that 'the family that eats together, stays together'. This is the importance you mentioned earlier about the dining table. That is the great focus, the socialising point of the house.

CH   I really do think you learn an awful lot by eating together. If you have never shared a table with anyone, you may not even be aware of small courtesies like passing the sugar to people. There was a wonderful survey carried out in Britain recently asking twelve-year-old children how you set a place on a table. There were many different responses, but the worrying thing was that 50 per cent didn't know, because they had never put a knife and fork on a table. They just picked up their meal, sat on the sofa and watched television.

JQ   We are not talking about old Victorian rules and etiquette here. It is more just the experience of being together as a family.

The following Family Project images by Elizabeth Handy were exhibited at Céifin Conference 2008

Photograph One – The Handys' House

First Family

Photograph Two – The Surrey Family

Photograph Three – The Surrey Family at Work

Photograph Four – The Surrey Family Caring

Photograph Five
– The Surrey Family Sharing

Second Family

Photograph Six – The Norfolk Family

Photograph Seven – The Norfolk Family at Work

Photograph Eight – The Norfolk Family Caring

Photograph Nine – The Norfolk Family Sharing

Third Family

Photograph Ten – The London Family

Photograph Eleven
– The London Family at Work

Photograph Twelve
– The London Family Caring

Photograph Thirteen – The London Family Sharing

The Handy Family

*Photograph Fourteen
— Liz's Different Roles*

*Photograph
Fifteen —
Charles' Role*

Still Life

Photograph Sixteen – Charles' Still Life

Photograph Seventeen – The Verity Family Still Life

Photograph Eighteen – The Aston Family

Photograph Nineteen – The Pearl Family

CH   Being together and realising that other people have needs, even if they're basic needs like wanting sugar or a glass of water, and that you have a responsibility to respond to those needs. They're very simple little things, but if you have never sat together and eaten together as a family you don't learn these things. Then you become incredibly selfish in a sense, because you've never had to take other people into account. You learn all of that at home, not at school.

JQ   You learn to communicate. There are messages in the way we say 'pass the sugar'.

CH   When I went to live in Windsor Castle I was surrounded by all these canons and priests. One of them leaned across the table to me once and said, 'Charles, would the Holy Spirit incline you to pass me the salt?' So you can ask for the salt in all sorts of different ways.

JQ   We are living in a more and more fragmented world, where community is fragmented and has almost disappeared in some cases, so the family is emerging as somewhere we can rightfully belong when all about us is collapsing.

CH   I know there are dysfunctional families and I know the best-selling autobiographies always start with, 'I had a hell of a childhood'. Mine unfortunately doesn't start with that, because I had a very nice childhood, but on the whole I think the family is the one great bastion that we can cling to in a very confusing world and we have to work at it. It doesn't come naturally or easily in many cases. Families are spread around the world these days, but they can be linked together by technology. And it doesn't take much every so often to hop on a plane and come together for some kind of family reunion, which I think is terribly important. I say in Chapter 15 of my book that I used to dread Elizabeth's family reunions, which happened every year. About twenty-five of her very strange family all gathered together, but it was actually extremely important. Now that her mother, who was the matriarch, has died, Elizabeth is assuming the matriarchal role and bringing them together. It is very important and much valued, though I think more often in retrospect than at the moment. We need to bring families together and we need to work at it, because it doesn't happen automatically.

JQ   Example really is the most powerful teacher of all is what you are getting at, more so than what we learn at school.

CH   I just watch our kids now, reaching the age of forty, and I see all sorts of things coming out in their behaviour that they must have learned in their teens and earlier from sitting in our home with us, even though we weren't teaching them. They learned from our example – both good and bad, I'm afraid to say – and it became deeply embedded in their customs, in the way they behave and in their values. I think if you are parents or grandparents now, beware! You are very potent people, even though you may not think it. You really are.

JQ   You make the point that fifteen years is now seen as the average length of a marriage in Britain. So you may end up having second families: step-sisters, step-brothers, half-sisters, half-brothers. There's a bit of adjustment to be made there.

CH Well, it's not that different. I was making the point that it was the length of marriage in Victorian times too. Only back then it ended because somebody died, usually the woman in childbirth. So when you said, 'For better or for worse, until death do us part,' that wasn't an awfully long way away. Now people leave after fifteen years, on average. Not in my case I'm afraid to say – maybe I would have had a more exciting life!

JQ However, you do make the point that you are on your second marriage, but to the same woman.

CH Everyone we know seems to be on a second marriage, so I say I'm on a second marriage too, but it's to the same woman. We radically revised our marriage contract when the kids left home, which is a time when you suddenly discover you haven't got that much to talk about because the family has dispersed and there are no squabbling children around. So what do you talk about? It was quite possible that with Elizabeth developing a career as a photographer and I developing a career as a writer, that we could have gone separate ways and no doubt eventually attached ourselves to another photographer and another writer. Instead we decided that we would work together, and in that way I was going to live with somebody that I worked with and vice versa. So we had, in a sense, a totally different kind of relationship, which was a second marriage in effect, but to the same woman. So I think you do need to adjust a marriage relationship as the family grows and changes and spreads out.

JQ I remember doing a series about retirement once and the wife in one case complained that she now had twice the husband and half the income. The first three months were hell because he kept asking her, 'What are we doing today?' He couldn't adjust. The whole notion of 'retirement', which I know you don't like as a word, can open up, or should open up, new possibilities.

CH   Retirement should be renamed reinvention, I think, and so then perhaps you should have a third marriage to the same woman or the same man, and rediscover the way you live together. Basically Elizabeth demanded that if we are going to have separate lives and separate careers, but bonded together, I should do my share of the rather more drudgery kind of work. So I do half the cooking and she does half the cooking. The only thing I don't seem to do is the clothes washing, I don't quite know why I don't, but otherwise we share everything.

JQ   About thirty years ago, you began writing about the future of work. To my mind you were way ahead of the pack. You were seeing how work would develop, how work would change, how we would work from home, the nature of work, how we would work, where we would work, how we would move out of work and back into it again. I would argue that your words have more or less come true. In terms of the family, which is what we are talking about here, could you look into your crystal ball and see what a family might be like in the future? What you would like it to be in thirty years from now?

CH   Well I think the dispersed family, the extended family, will be different. It won't so much be uncles and aunts and cousins, it will be steps and halves and even friends, close friends who become sort of welded into the family. They will possibly be extended physically and geographically around the world, but linked increasingly by technology, and there will be grand and wonderful reunions every so often when they all come together. I think that the family will increase in importance because of the chaotic nature of the world that we are entering. Nobody will belong to anything. Organisations will be very much short-term relationships. Organisations don't remember you, organisations don't say thank you, and you are only useful to organisations while you're there. They used to be a place to which you committed your loyalty and, indeed, your life. When I started off I joined an oil company and it was generally expected that I would be there for my whole life. They also said, when I retired, statistically I would only live another eighteen months because life after Shell would be unendurable. It is not like that anymore, so don't put your faith in organisations. Put your faith in physical communities; because people are moving so much, where on earth do you belong to in the end? In the end, I do believe it is only the family. You have to work at it, it doesn't happen automatically; living with people is very difficult. You have to organise these family get-togethers and you have to organise the communication. When I went abroad to South-East Asia, my mother and my father wrote to me nearly every week. Did I write back to them? About once every three months. Now I realise how much agony I must have caused them because I was in way-off places they had never heard of like Borneo, and all they got back was silence. I wasn't working at it; I should have been, but until you become a parent yourself you don't understand these things.

JQ   And the spaces those families will occupy? Ideally, how do you see the homes of the future?

CH   I'm not very optimistic; we'll see what the architects say when we talk to them about such matters. It seems to me that homes are getting smaller and smaller and smaller, and it is incredibly difficult to have any kind of extended family physically living there. We are trying to say, look, you can do the sort of thing we're doing, you can give people their separate space in the same compound, as it were. But when our children choose to go, as one of them did to go live in New Zealand for seven years, what do you do about it? Email helps of course, but it also meant that we had to get on an airplane once a year and go and see her, which was not pleasant. So I worry about the physical space. I don't know what the architects are going to say and I would dearly like to see more arrangements like the one we have, which is a big house subdivided into family units. Families matter most and families need working at. Families are the schoolrooms for life, for children, and the rest-homes for old age.

JQ   And they need to be celebrated?

CH   They need to be celebrated: celebrated by society and helped by society, if society can find ways of doing it, and celebrated by the families themselves. Rituals are important, celebrations are important.

Relationships

A New Vision for the Changing Family

John Yzaguirre, Ph.D.
Psychologist, Educator and Author

Introduction

Family life has changed dramatically over the last few decades in the US, as indicated by increased social approval of alternatives to traditional family life, increased separation between marriage and parenthood, increased tolerance for non-marital cohabitation and an increase in single parent families. Studies on marital happiness show that in the last decades there has been a decline in marital happiness, less marital interaction, more marital conflict and more work-related stress. On the other hand, we are witnessing the emergence of the Marriage Movement, a grass-roots movement to strengthen marriage and reduce divorce and unwed childbearing. For a detailed description of changes in family life in the US in the last fifty years, please refer to the resources listed at the end of this chapter. The following is a brief summary of the most significant ones.

Two New Child-Free Adult Life Stages

Today, 32% of households have children (the lowest percentage in US history) versus 50% in 1960. This reflects a shift from a child-centered marriage to a 'soul-mate' marriage. Marriage today is seen primarily as an emotional and sexual partnership and there is an increasing separation of parenthood from marriage. The current tendency is to see marriage as a couple's relationship designed to fulfill the emotional needs of adults, rather than an institution dedicated to raising children. The US is shifting from a society of child-rearing families to a society of child-free adults. In a representative survey of US adults published in 2007, 75% said that the main purpose of marriage was the mutual happiness and fulfillment of adults rather than raising children. We are witnessing a growing population of affluent singles, childless couples and empty nesters. The life stages before and after having children are no longer seen as brief transitional stages that precede or follow the most significant period of parenthood. They are now portrayed as two distinct and separate stages in the adult life course. The focus in these two new 'child-free' stages is on self-improvement and self-investment. People in these stages are highly valued as workers and consumers. The stage before children continues to expand since women delay marriage to get more schooling and work experience and they wait longer before they bear their first child. The stage after children also expands due to lower fertility rates and the extension of adult life expectancy with greater health.

Increase in Non-Marital Cohabitation

Another significant change in family life has been the sharp increase in the number of cohabiting couples: people who are sexual partners, not married to each other and sharing a household. Over 50% of all first marriages are now preceded by living together versus virtually none 50 years ago, and 10% of couples are cohabiting today. It is estimated that 40% of all children will spend some time in a cohabiting household during their growing up years. Studies in non-marital cohabitation indicate that those who live together before marriage are more likely to break up after marriage.

Increase in Single-Parent Families

The trend toward single-parent families is having a major impact on children and adolescents today. Children in such families have negative life outcomes at two to three times the rate of children in married or two-parent families. In 2007, 28% of families were single-parent families versus 9% in 1960, and 37% of children were born to unmarried women versus 5% in 1960. The number of never-married single mothers is now higher than that of divorced single mothers.

Children at Greater Risk

The increasing numbers of children being born and living with single parents or unstable cohabiting couples, and the high number of children experiencing the divorce of their parents is leading to a generation of children and adolescents at a higher risk for mental, emotional, behavioural and health problems. In 2000, 34% of children lived apart from their biological fathers versus 17% in 1960. Research studies consistently show that the psychosocial well-being of children and adolescents increases when they grow up in a household with biological parents who have a healthy marriage. To help children and adolescents overcome the emotional impoverishment resulting from the lack of stable and nurturing family connections, we need to help parents establish and sustain healthy marriages.

Teenagers' Attitudes about Marriage and Family

There is a significant increase in the acceptance of alternative lifestyles to marriage by young people today. Only 63% of today's highschool seniors expect to be married to the same person for life, 62% think that living together before marriage is a good idea and 53% accept out-of-wedlock childbearing as a 'worthwhile lifestyle'.

Family Life Today: The Greatest Revolution?

The Marriage Movement

On a more positive note, we are witnessing the emergence of the Marriage Movement, a grass-roots movement to strengthen marriage and to reduce divorce and unwed childbearing. This movement includes, but is not limited to, the following programmes: marriage education, research-based, faith-based, school-based and healthy marriage initiatives.

Education Programmes

Marriage education programmes focus on developing the knowledge and skills for making a wise marital choice and having a successful marriage. A very influential example is The Coalition for Marriage, Family and Couples Education (CMFCE). It was created in 1996 by mental health professionals, researchers, clergy and policy advocates. Its directory of programmes has increased from 15 in 1997 to 140 in 2000. For further information you can visit: www.smartmarriages.com.

Research-Based Programmes

David Popenoe and Barbara Dafoe Whitehead established the research-oriented National Marriage Project at Rutgers University in 1997. They publish an annual report: *The State of Our Unions: The Social Health of Marriage in America*. Several well-known researchers at different universities have created family institutes and research labs that provide research-based findings on marriage and family life, for example: John Gottman at the University of Washington; Howard Markman, Scott Stanley and Susan Blumberg at the University of Denver; Andrew Christiansen and Thomas Bradbury at UCLA; David Olson at the University of Minnesota. The Couples and Marriage Policy Resource Center provides technical assistance and consultation to national, state and community leaders. It has a special focus on helping low-income and welfare populations. In 1995, The Council on Families, a non-partisan and interdisciplinary group of family scholars and writers, released *Marriage in America: A Report to the Nation*.

Faith-Based Programmes

The National Pastoral Initiative for Marriage was launched by the US Catholic Bishops in 2005 to offer guidance and resources aimed at promoting, strengthening, sustaining and restoring marriages. For more information visit: www.foryourmarriage.org.

The Covenant Marriage Movement, a new, non-political, Church-based group made by 31 million people from 35 national Christian organisations was created in 1999. They plan to hold events in major cities to sign a renewed vow to God, each other, their families and their communities. Leaders of the US Catholic Church, the National Council of Churches, the Southern Baptist Convention and the National Association of Evangelicals reached a groundbreaking ecumenical agreement in 2000 to work together to strengthen marriage. They created an ecumenical ad campaign promoting marriage and endorsed a World Marriage Day. The growth of Marriage Savers, a lay ministry headed by Harriet and Mike McManus, has helped 5,500 clergy in 125 cities organise Community Marriage Policies and Covenants. Clergy agree to require engaged couples to undergo four months of marriage preparation, encourage marriage enrichment and intervention programmes such as Marriage Encounter, Family Life Weekends or Retrouvaille, create stepfamily support groups and train lay mentor couples to help engaged couples, newlyweds and troubled marriages.

Family Life Today: The Greatest Revolution?

School-Based Programmes

As many as 1,000 schools in 35 states include marriage education within life skills, family life, domestic science, health, teen pregnancy and abstinence education classes. In 1998 Florida became the first state to mandate marriage and relationship skills training in all public and private high schools.

The Healthy Marriage Initiative

The Administration for Children and Families within the Department of Health and Human Services launched the Healthy Marriage Initiative in 2002, to support programmes designed to help couples form and sustain healthy marriages with an emphasis on providing strong and stable environments for raising children. These programmes are carried out in coordination with many public-, faith- and community-based organisations and private partners. They work with 225 different groups and have provided grants for the amount of over $150 million. A Marriage Resource Center was established in 2004 as a clearinghouse of information for the general public, practitioners, policy makers and researchers: www.healthymarriageinfo.org.

New Vision: Focus on Relationships of Mutuality

In the midst of the critical changes in family life that we have witnessed in the last few decades, a significant search for greater emotional connection and intimacy is emerging. Couples are searching for a new vision on how to achieve lasting and mutually rewarding relationships. The positive impact of the Marriage Movement on marital satisfaction and family strength, as well as the new cultural trend to integrate values of commitment over market values, gives us reasons to be optimistic about the future of the family. The good news is that successful marriages are skill-based and value-driven, and there is increasing empirical evidence that couples can learn skills and acquire values in many different formats and settings and that the benefits persist over time. Through our research and over 25 years of clinical practice with couples and families, my wife and I have developed a vision of the family as a school of relationships of mutuality that sustain family unity. We have created an education programme that teaches family members three skill sets involved in the dynamics of unity: empathy, autonomy and mutuality. Empathy skills involve learning to accept others as they are, to understand their needs, and to love them concretely as they want to be loved. Autonomy skills are understood as developing a healthy self that does not ignore, dominate or submit to others, but relates with others in a cooperative and egalitarian way. In the US there are three prevailing socio-cultural trends that threaten the development of a healthy self: secular individualism, restless activism and excessive consumerism. We propose three antidotes for them: a relational understanding of self, freedom from time famine and enjoying a simpler lifestyle. Empathy and autonomy are necessary to achieve mutuality, but they are not sufficient. Mutuality requires interactive skills that aim at building and strengthening relationships and restoring them when needed. The essential skills of mutuality include conflict-free communication, integrating personal differences and restoring unity.

Interactive Styles

If we grouped the interactive styles between family members into basic categories, we could describe the primary ones as falling into one of the following groups: individualism, dominance, codependency or mutuality.

Family members whose primary interactive style is individualistic focus primarily on their personal needs with disregard for the needs of others. In the dynamics between 'you' and 'I', there is an invisible barrier that we can call indifference, neglect or avoidance. Obviously people with this social orientation fail to generate meaningful relationships with others and often suffer from isolation and loneliness. They act as if they are the only important person.

People with a dominant interactive style are very aware of others because they are trying to control them and/or impose their views on them. These people act as if they are more important than other family members. They might be aware of the needs of others, but they focus primarily on fulfilling their own needs first. They often exhibit discriminatory attitudes and behaviours that prevent or inhibit the development of mutually rewarding interactions with others.

People with a codependent interactive style act as if they are less important than others. They often try to please others, putting aside their own needs, in order to gain much wanted acceptance and approval from them. They often lose their own identity and assimilate themselves into what they perceive the dominant people want from them.

What individualism, dominance and codependency have in common is that they fail to build healthy relationships. People with an interactive style, which focuses on mutuality, experience something new: they are able to integrate the 'you' and 'I' into an egalitarian and interdependent 'we', which transcends both and fulfills them. This is the only approach that gives equal importance to the needs of others and to personal needs. How do we promote mutuality in the interactions among family members? By promoting the following sets of skills and values.

Empathy: Radical Acceptance

Accepting others as they are

To build authentic relationships at home, the first step is to open yourself to others and welcome them as they are, without trying to change or control them. We are all a 'work in progress' and accepting each other with our limitations does not mean that we settle for mediocrity or stagnation, but that we create the conditions for voluntary personal change and ongoing growth. When people feel accepted they often become open to change, however, when they feel coerced or negatively judged they often become defensive and resistant to change.

Understanding their needs

How do you know what other family members need from you? Just ask them in a timely and sincere manner. Be realistic about what you can do and when you can do it. There are three universal needs that you can meet almost daily; we call them the 'Triple A': attention, affection and appreciation:

- Need for attention: through your personal interest, make others feel important.
- Need for affection: through your shows of affection, make others feel lovable.
- Need for appreciation: through your praise, make others feel special and valued.

Loving others concretely as they want to be loved

If you ask other family members, with genuine interest, how they want to be loved, they will tell you. If you respond by treating them as they want to be treated, they will feel loved and prone to reciprocate your love. One of the greatest tragedies we witness in couples' therapy is to see two people who care for each other show their love in non-meaningful or irrelevant ways, and instead of being happy they are miserable with each other.

To summarise, radical acceptance involves three essential steps: (1) welcoming others as they are by emptying ourselves and making room for them in our lives; (2) understanding their needs by becoming interested in their lives and identifying with them; (3) loving others concretely as they want to be loved. The first two steps show our sensitivity to others and the last one our responsiveness. Our level of sensitivity and responsiveness determine the strength of our emotional bond with them.

Autonomy: the Gift of a Healthy Self

Autonomy is understood here as developing a healthy self that does not ignore, dominate or submit to others, but relates with others in a cooperative way. We propose three strategies to develop a healthy self: a relational understanding of self, freedom from time famine and enjoying a simpler lifestyle.

A relational understanding of self
The self is often defined according to individual attributes, skills and intrapersonal characteristics, which differentiate us from other people. A primary objective for the self in a culture of secular individualism is self-fulfillment and independence. We propose that our true self can be fully expressed when we relate with others in relationships characterised by equality and mutuality. This relational view of self allows us to move from being self-centered to becoming inter-connected with others. It frees us from feelings of isolation, loneliness and emotional distance from others. What defines us is not what we have or what we do, but how we relate with others. This relational understanding of self leads to an experience of unity with others while maintaining our own identity.

Freedom from time famine

Most adults in the US are time-starved, stressed out, sleep-deprived, overworked and under-exercised. These conditions prevent or inhibit the process of self-giving and often create an attitude of self-preservation, hostility (perceiving others as a threat to our well-being) or dependency (needing or wanting others to take care of us).

We need to shift from living in a crisis management mode, characterised by endless multitasking and rushing, and move into living a balanced life, centered on living meaningfully in the present moment. The art of living in the present mindfully and heartfully is receiving increasing attention in the field of psychology. Adults need to master time and stress management strategies to prevent the job getting the best of them and the family getting the leftovers. In our book, *Thriving Marriages,* we have a chapter called 'The House of Self', where we describe how to integrate the seven essential dimensions of life in order to enjoy balance and personal growth.

Enjoying a simpler lifestyle

David Myers, a well-known social psychologist, wrote about the American paradox wherein the more stuff we accumulate the less joy we seem to experience. The buying power of people in the US more than doubled from the 1950s through to the 1990s, and yet people did not report feeling significantly happier. We propose replacing the market values of excessive consumption, supersizing and immediate gratification with a culture of sharing, which encourages the praxis of giving to the poor what we do not use or need, buying only what we need and sharing what we have (for example, talents, knowledge, skills, time, possessions, money, etc.). When we declutter our lives and develop a simpler lifestyle, we experience more personal joy and benefit the community.

Mutuality: Dynamics of Sharing

We have seen how empathy skills can make other members in our family feel welcomed, understood and cared for. Our autonomy skills give us the initiative to share the best of us with them freely and willingly. Empathy and autonomy bring us closer to each other. Where is the meeting place between 'you' and 'I'? It is the 'living space' created by our mutuality skills. Empathy and autonomy are necessary to achieve mutuality, but they are not sufficient. Mutuality requires interactive skills that aim at building and strengthening relationships and at restoring them when needed. The essential skills of mutuality include: conflict-free communication, integrating personal differences and restoring unity.

Conflict-free communication

Couples today are struggling with lack of time for their personal sharing and when they get together they are prone to spend their sharing time trying to solve their conflicts. To remove these inhibitors so that authentic communication can be experienced, we invite couples to establish rituals of personal communication where they share meaningful personal experiences without complaining, venting, criticising or engaging in problem-solving.

This type of communication produces mutual understanding and validation and deepens the level of emotional and spiritual intimacy among them. For many couples this means setting aside some time each day to enjoy emotionally safe, conflict-free sharing.

Integrating personal differences

One of the main differences between successful couples and those who break up is not the type of conflicts that they face but how they deal with them. Unsuccessful couples end up using a fight, flight or freeze response to conflict. In a fight response they attack their partner through blaming, criticising, shaming, ridiculing, trivialising or with verbal or physical abuse. In a flight response they try to defend themselves from their partner by engaging in such behaviours as justifying themselves, withdrawing, avoiding their partner or talking about the conflict, isolating, giving the 'silent treatment' or making empty promises. In a freeze response they become paralysed and usually play the victim or submit passively to their partner's requests. None of these approaches succeed at solving conflicts. Since the majority of marital conflicts are caused by the differences between the spouses and not by major pathological impairments, we teach couples how to integrate their differences with wisdom and respect. We call this approach the 'UVA' response (Understand, Value and Act). First, we teach couples to achieve adequate emotional control to be able to dialogue respectfully, then the speaker:

- Defines the conflict in behavioural terms: 'When you … I feel …'
- Defines the solution in concrete and positive terms: 'Next time I would prefer that you …'

The listener responds with a 'UVA' response:

- Understanding the spouse's need or expectation: 'Let me see if I understood …'
- Valuing what the spouse wants or needs, even if he or she disagrees with it.
- Acting: committing to a specific and relevant behaviour, out of love for the spouse.

This approach allows them to feel understood, valued and loved, and results in a deeper experience of intimacy.

Restoring unity

Nobody can love perfectly 24/7. Sooner or later the experience of mutuality is disrupted by some painful or unfair event that calls for forgiveness and reconciliation. When we forgive we are saying: 'I forgive you because who you are is more important to me than what you did'. Forgiveness is a healing process involving our soul (loving as God loves), mind (restoring the dignity and positive view of the offender), heart (cancelling the emotional debt) and will (initiating the behavioural changes needed to restore justice). Forgiveness activates mercy and reconciliation restores justice in the relationship. The process of restoring unity in the relationship needs to integrate mercy and justice.

From Vision to Action

Share the good news about healthy families

There is strong empirical evidence that a good marriage enhances personal happiness, economic success, health and longevity. Married men and women in all age groups are more likely to be healthier both physically as well as emotionally than single, separated, divorced or widowed individuals. Research findings indicate that children and youth who are raised by parents in healthy marriages are physically and emotionally healthier, more likely to achieve greater academic success, less likely to exhibit major behavioural problems, less likely to use alcohol and drugs and less likely to be raised in poverty than those raised by parents in unhealthy marriages. Today's young people want strong intimate relationships and we can show them that healthy marriages and families are the best way to achieve it.

Promote a new vision for the changing family

We need to move beyond a self-centered culture that values independence, individual gratification and short-term personal gain, and move towards an interconnected culture that values mutuality as a new way to achieve self-fulfillment, long-term meaningful relationships and community well-being. Most people, including unmarried parents, value marriage and want to be married. Children thrive best when raised by both biological married parents, as long as the marriage is healthy.

A review of decades of marital research suggests that healthy marriages have in common high levels of commitment, marital satisfaction, good communication and conflict-resolution skills, emotional intimacy and fidelity. In other words, healthy marriages and families are those who develop and sustain healthy relationships.

Here I have presented a new vision on how to achieve family unity by teaching empathy, autonomy and mutuality skills, and by embracing such values as long-term commitment, radical acceptance, relational self-fulfillment, sharing, intimacy and unity.

Expand education and support programmes

Given the prevailing socio-cultural trends that weaken marriages and families, we need to promote healthy marriages and strong families in all levels of society by expanding educational and support programmes. There are many effective and user-friendly programmes that can train marriage and family educators in major social 'portals', such as churches, highschools, hospitals and community centers. For a complete directory of programmes visit: www.smartmarriages.com.

The empirical evaluations of marriage education programmes indicate that they are both well received and have generally positive and lasting outcomes.

For those who might be interested in using the Thriving Marriages programme, I recommend reading our book,

Thriving Marriages, for a detailed description of its components or to contact the authors at www.ThrivingFamilies.com. Thriving Marriages uses the 'RIPE' approach: relevant, inspirational, practical and effective.

- Relevant because it responds to the most critical needs of families today by offering a vision and praxis for building unity in the family.
- Inspirational because it integrates empirically-based research findings with a contemporary spirituality of unity.
- Practical because it has immediate and concrete application as part of a premarital preparation, marriage enrichment, parenting education and/or healthy lifestyle programme.
- Effective because those who apply it consistently report significant and lasting positive changes.

We are optimistic about the future of the changing family because we are witnessing the powerful development of a Marriage Movement, which provides quality education programmes that strengthen families, and because most people want to learn the skills and live the values involved in building unity in the family.

Resources

Child Trends Research Brief, *What is 'Healthy Marriage':
Defining the Concept*, Washington, DC: Child Trends, 2004.
www.childtrends.org.

Coalition for Marriage, Family and Couples Education;
Institute for American Values; Religion, Culture, and Family
Project, University of Chicago Divinity School, *The Marriage
Movement: A Statement of Principles*, New York City: Institute
for American Values, 2000.

Doherty, William, *Take Back Your Marriage: Sticking Together in a
World That Pulls Us Apart*, New York: The Guilford Press, 2001.

Halford, K., Markman, H., Kline, G. and Stanley S., 'Best
Practice in Couple Relationship Education', *Journal of Marital
and Family Therapy*, Vol. 29, No. 3 (July 2003), pp. 385–406.

Myers, David, *The American Paradox: Spiritual Hunger in an Age
of Plenty*, New Haven: Yale University Press, 2000.

National Healthy Marriage Resource Center:
www.healthymarriageinfo.org.

National Pastoral Initiative on Marriage by the US Conference
of Catholic Bishops:
www.usccb.org/bishops/pastoralinitiative.htm
and www.foryourmarriage.org.

Pew Research Centre Reports on Family and Relationships
from 2005 to 2008: www.pewsocialtrends.org.

Smart Marriages, The Coalition for Marriage, Family and
Couples Education: www.smartmarriages.com.

Sollee, Diane, *The Emerging Field of Marriage Education: Creating Smart Marriage for the Millennium*, Coalition for Marriage, Family and Couples Education, 2000.

The Healthy Marriage Initiative:
www.acf.hhs.gov/healthymarriage

The National Marriage Project, *The State of Our Unions: The Social Health of Marriage in America*, Rutgers, the State University of New Jersey: The National Marriage Project, 2003, 2004, 2005, 2006, 2007, 2008.

Waite, L.J. and Gallagher, M., *The Case for Marriage: Why Married People Are Happier, Healthier, and Better Off Financially*, New York: Doubleday, 2000.

Yzaguirre, John and Frazier-Yzaguirre, Claire, *Thriving Marriages: An Inspirational and Practical Guide to Lasting Happiness*, New York: New City Press, 2004.

Notes from the Chair

Ciana Campbell,
Broadcaster and Media Consultant

Having a November birthday means for me that the month combines celebration and reflection: celebration that I'm still alive and kicking and reflection on the year past and the time ahead. November 2008 brought a little more reflection than usual because there was a great, big zero attached to my age. The Céifin session, which I was to chair, came just a week before I was due to turn the great half-century, and it was the perfect trigger for thoughts of how those decades had shaped me and what I could hope for in the future.

Joining me on the panel to tell their stories were three people who have almost one hundred years of parenting experience between them: mother, grandmother and Honorary President of Age & Opportunity, Mamo McDonald; stay-at-home dad and former financial journalist, Kevin Murphy; and Geraldine Reidy, a mother who has also represented Lone Parent Groups in Ireland.

All three have an extraordinary list of personal and professional achievements to their credit. Mamo was widowed when her eleven children were still quite young; she then had to become the family breadwinner. She became well known in Ireland for her leadership of the Irish Countrywomen's Association in the 1980s and has also been an advocate for the rights of older people for many years.

Family Life Today: The Greatest Revolution?

Kevin Murphy has been a stay-at-home dad for the past twelve years; prior to that he had been a financial journalist. He has combined his time at home with returning to education and qualifying as a psychotherapist. He now has a part-time practice and also volunteers in one of the State prisons as well as with Parentline.

Our third panelist, Geraldine, raised her two children alone following the break-up of her marriage twenty-five years ago and now advocates for and trains other lone parents. I knew that the conference organisers had pure gold on their hands – this would be a rich and diverse panel from whom we could all learn.

It was not my first time to chair the 'Telling My Story' session and I was delighted to be invited back. This session is particularly important because, to me, these stories are the very beating heart of a Céifin conference. It is, of course, vital that we have overviews, studies and reports, and any exploration of family life requires academic research and policy reviews, but unless we hear the individual stories of love and pain, of heartbreak and joy, of dreams and reality, then we do the subject a disservice.

Families may come in all shapes and sizes, they may be places of safety and care or of fear and abuse, but they are our starting point, our launching pad in life, and to fully understand the range of families in Ireland we must hear from those at the coalface. However, this session also requires an enormous degree of trust. If you are asked to tell your own personal story you must believe that you will be treated with respect and that your narrative will be valued.

Part of my role as Chair is to build that trust and to ensure that speakers know what to expect from the session. Through emails and phone calls we discuss and plan in the month prior to the conference. Some things are straightforward, such as the speaking order or technical requirements, but others take time.

Stories unfold and very personal details emerge. I ask virtual strangers to entrust me with the intimate details of their lives and it is probably a mark of their trust in the Céifin organisation that they do. They believe in the value of the conference and in their contribution to the exploration of values and ethics. We should all be grateful for their participation.

The 2008 conference was no exception: Mamo, Kevin and Geraldine brought us through their stories and reflected on how lives could be improved through their knowledge and experience. Geraldine did a terrific piece on lobbying for changes in government policy during the question and answer time; Mamo took us on a journey of parenting through the decades, bringing us bang up-to-date with a very funny anecdote describing how her grandchild was briefly babysat across two continents through Skype; and Kevin graphically described the isolation that stay-at-home parents can feel. Their overall message was one of cherishing the time spent with our children and grandchildren and of celebrating diversity in family shape and structure.

It was a privilege to spend time in their company. My own family commitments meant that I wasn't able to linger after the session ended, and I was unable to attend the conference dinner. I had swimmers to pick up and feed, homework to check and a sick relative to nurse. However, energised by the session, I knew that I was extraordinarily lucky to have those cares and that I did have much to celebrate for my fifty years. Thank you Céifin for the reminder.

Telling My Story Panel Discussion
Family Life and Parenting

With facilitator, Ciana Campbell, and panelists,
Mamo McDonald, Kevin Murphy and
Geraldine Reidy

Ciana Campbell

This session is particularly important because these stories, in a sense, are at the beating heart of the Céifin Conferences. To fully understand the range of families in Ireland we are delighted to have three people on the panel to tell their very rich stories: Mamo McDonald, Kevin Murphy and Geraldine Reidy.

The first panel member, Mamo McDonald, is a mother of eleven children and now grandmother to thirty-two grandchildren, at the last count, and has one great-grandchild. Mamo became well-known in Ireland and beyond for her leadership of the Irish Countrywomen's Association in the 1980s. Mamo has been working on ageing issues since 1987 when she chaired Ireland's first National Day of Ageing, an initiative which led to the setting up of Age & Opportunity. She was Age & Opportunity's Chairperson for many years and is now Honorary President. She won a very well-deserved People of the Year Award for her leadership in that role. One of the projects that is closest to Mamo's heart is the Bealtaine Festival, which takes place every May, celebrating creativity in older age. She has been a member of various committees on ageing, including the National Steering Committee of The United Nations International Year of Older Persons in 1999. She has been the driving force behind OWN, a national network that seeks to be a voice for older women, of which she is on the board of directors.

At seventy, she went to university to study for a Higher Diploma and a Masters Degree in Women's Studies, and in 2004 she was awarded a Certificate in Ageing and Equality from UCD. They are extraordinary achievements by any stretch of the imagination, but even more so when you consider that Mamo was widowed when her children were still quite young, leaving her to provide for her children, as well as literally playing the role of both mother and father in the family. Mamo wants to bring her perspective on family life and parenting in Ireland to the Céifin Conference.

Mamo McDonald

I am going to start with a little verse, I write some poetry and this is one my family say embarrass them at all sorts of occasions:

> My family was fifties born, all six of them
> And then there followed '62, 3, 4, 6 and 7
> Today we celebrate the birthday of a '60s son
> And raise a glass to Billings – him be fiddlesticks!

The thing is, we never would have sent any of them back. Thirty years ago, the St John of God's Order celebrated one hundred years in Ireland and I was invited to give a talk on 'The Family of the Future'. I looked down the list of speakers and, daunted by the calibre of the people, I set to studying and researching and writing and rewriting. I had a friend called Fr Seamus and I called him into the kitchen one day and said, 'Sit down there. I want to try out this paper on you'. So I read my paper, which a lot of blood, sweat and tears had gone into, and at the end he said, 'Very good, very good'. So I said, 'But what's wrong with it'? He replied, 'Why do you think you were asked to write this paper?' 'Well, I suppose it's because I have eleven children and I would be seen to have a certain expertise'. 'That's it,' he said, 'so why are you giving other people's? Maybe you should talk a little about yourself and your experience.' That was the first time I learned that the personal is political.

The Chinese have a proverb, 'To prophesy is extremely difficult, especially with respect to the future', and as you know I was writing this paper on 'the Family of the Future'. I was in the thick of family life at the time, with very few of them gone off the top, as we say, and a lot of them still at school at all levels. Being an optimist, I was looking forward to a future of 'happy-ever-aftering', with my husband and I walking hand-in-hand into the sunset together. Exactly four weeks to the day from when I read that paper I found Eugene, my husband, lying dead on the golf course in Clones and everything changed.

There were no counselling services at that time, so I had to deal with the devastation and the loss on my own, as best I could. As I saw after a while, I was left with two alternatives: one was to sink and the other was to survive. I chose survival, because there was a job the two of us had started and only me left now to get on with it. There were many rocky patches, particularly with some of the boys in the middle of the family who were in their mid-teens, and the loss of their father was particularly relevant for them and I felt that for a while that they lost direction. Fortunately, they found their way again, but at that time they were flexing their muscles against authority and they resented any intervention from older siblings. That was one of the particularly difficult things. I was at the doctor around that time and he said to me, 'I know the stresses you have to deal with, I have eight myself and they are no better or worse than anyone elses'. It was actually consoling to have that said to me.

Women of my time gave up paid work when we married; we *had* to by law. There were other laws which made life difficult for women; for instance, the law of domicile. If your husband should head off to Ulaan Bator or Timbuktu, that was your domicile, even though you might never have left the parish at all. There was the law of criminal conversation, which wasn't repealed until the 1980s, and that stated that if a woman's affections were drawn away from her husband, he could claim financial compensation from the seducer for the loss of the services of his wife. However, she didn't have reciprocal rights with regards to him. There was a family law which meant that your house could be sold without your knowledge, let alone your consent. However, it wasn't those big things that you were thinking of, it was that you were working eighty hours a week and there was no pay – it was unpaid work so it wasn't counted in the Gross National Product. Having to ask for the price of a hairdo or a pair of stockings, or worse still having to ask for money to buy your husband a birthday present, could take the glamour off family life. When the law on working was changed and women could continue to work, the 'laying hen', as they say, was very popular. Up around my country the teachers and nurses were particularly prized. Becoming part of the European Union was good for women beacuse a lot of these laws were being changed as the European influence came into being.

I was thinking about other changes that have happened during my lifetime of being a parent and, out of all of them, I think the best change is husbands being present at the birth of their children. I think that was an enormous change because, first of all, it gave husbands a greater appreciation of their wives, it bonded them more, but it particularly bonded fathers with their children. I know that each of my sons, and I have nine of them, all cited that as one of the most amazing moments of their lives, to be present at the birth of their children. I loved the sharing of the parenting duties where the women, for instance, learned how to change fuses and men how to change nappies. In all the nineteen years of nappy changing in my house, Eugene never changed one. So this was a great thing, these interchangeable roles and the whole involvement in rearing the children.

This is the age of communication, we are told, and it has a good side and a bad side where family life is concerned. I think children tend to be more open with their parents, they tend to ask questions that certainly we never would have dared. What isn't good about it is this constant need to be in communication with one another if they are not actually together; children text one another and that can be very annoying. The whole area of being able to find things on the internet has huge value, particularly for finding out and researching topics that they are interested in; the bad side is that they so often have unsupervised access to television and the internet.

I think another negative aspect of life today is the sexualisation of children before they are ready for it. Television, magazines and all these different chat rooms – all these things tend to instil a sexual appetite into children before they are even fit to make their own meals. I have lived through this whole throwaway phase when everything was 'cheap, cheery and chuckable'; everything is disposable and consumerism became the god of a certain generation. Hopefully, with this new downturn in the economy, we might revert back to conservation and recycling, and more attention will be given to preserving and enhancing the ties that bind.

One lesson I have learned is that there is no retirement from being a parent. The good news is that adult relationships with children are very enriching and a great source of joy, as are the wonders and challenges of being a grandparent. As I said, I have thirty-two grandchildren: sixteen granddaughters and sixteen grandsons, which I think is a nice balance considering I had nine sons and two daughters, so things have evened up a bit.

Recently I have enjoyed things with grandchildren like card painting and making jewellery from melon seeds, which my grandmother taught me how to do. We have made pancakes and sometimes we have a doughnut session, where they make doughnuts with me and then we have a doughnut orgy for lunch. That sort of thing is the great joy of my life now.

Recently I heard of another advancement. My son, Donald, was sitting in his home in Millbrook in Clones and he was talking on Skype to his daughter-in-law and grandson in Chico, California. For some reason Rachel needed to go down to say something to the janitor of the apartment block where she was living. So she said to Donald, 'Would you keep an eye on Dylan for me, you have my mobile number and if I'm needed just tell me, and I'll be back in a second'.

I will finish by quoting Nell McCafferty, who once said, 'A family proves that you can love anybody and it provides you with a ringside seat on the great events of life'.

Our next panel member, Kevin Murphy, has been a stay-at-home dad for the past twelve years, and prior to that he was a financial journalist with the Irish Independent. *He lives in Dublin with his three teenage children and his wife Gina Quin, who is Chief Executive of the Dublin Chamber of Commerce. During his time at home he has been a regular contributor to media discussions and debates on fatherhood and parenting in general. Kevin holds a degree in Psychology, a Masters of Science Degree in Investment and Treasury and a Master of Science Degree in Psychoanalytic Psychotherapy. Whilst still at home, he is a practising psychotherapist in Dublin and he arranges his working hours around the needs of his family. He is a volunteer psychotherapist in one of the State prisons and a volunteer with Parentline, a helpline that offers a listening service to parents under stress. He is also the author of* It's a Dad's Life, *a book about being a stay-at-home parent, which is based on a humorous column he wrote for a Sunday newspaper for seven years. Just in case you didn't think he had any time for himself, his hobby is middle-distance sea swimming. Kevin can obviously bring a whole slew of perspectives as a parent, as a support to other parents and, of course, as a stay-at-home father.*

Kevin Murphy

Thank you for the nice introduction. I do sea swimming just to get a bit of peace and quiet, it's the only place that the phone doesn't ring and I can think to myself. I'd like to say well done to Mamo, I thoroughly enjoyed her talk. I met Mamo for the first time over lunch at the conference and it turns out that I worked with one of her sons in the 1980s, so it is a small world indeed. If I could begin with something that Mamo mentioned: this new trend for men to be at the birth of their children. With our first child I was not just at the birth, I was also there for the breaking of the waters, which was quite a traumatic event for the first child. We were at a wedding in Kilcullen of a very good friend of mine. He was up at the altar and as the bride came up the aisle, all hell broke loose. I said, 'We can't leave now; she's just coming up the aisle'. We had to sit there as water emerged around our ankles until the moment that the bride passed our pew, and then we made a dash for it and no one in the church knew what was happening. They thought we were having a row, I suspect. We got to the hospital and everything went fine; our first child, Alice, arrived. A week later the bride and groom had a party with all the people who had been at the wedding because we had missed the reception. I ended up talking to a woman who had been sitting behind us and, as we had left the church, she didn't know what was going on and had turned to her husband and said, 'You know these old churches – you think they would fix the roof'. And her husband said, 'Why?' And she looked upwards and then down at the floor. That is a true story, but the main point is that I was present at the birth of my children.

That was in 1996 and we had two more daughters after that, three girls in total. I suppose I was a very career-focused person up to that point, and the pattern set out for us by the time we had our first and second and third child was that the children would go into a crèche and we would both go back to work to pay for the mortgage and for this and for that. However, neither of us felt comfortable with that, and as number two and number three came along we became even less and less enamoured with this way of life. At the time my wife had a job where she travelled a lot around the country and I had a job that required working late into the evening because it was in a newspaper, and we were getting in babysitters to let the childminder go home, who would pick them up from the crèche. It was very complicated and very unsatisfactory.

For quite a number of years we would always be doing a sum on the back of an envelope to work out what it would mean if one of us stayed at home. Could we afford to do that? The eldest was seven before the figure that came out at the end actually said, yes – we could get away with this. Maybe one of us could stay at home and, of course, I was earning slightly less at the time and I had a job where I could do a little bit on the part-time side. This didn't apply to my wife, so I was the one who stayed at home. I have to say that the figure that came out on the envelope was a complete miscalculation; it was much more expensive than we had thought! But we got by and I'm twelve years down the road now of being the stay-at-home dad. If Charles Handy needs to know how to work the washing machine, or to iron, or to shop, he can call me. I find it a very enriching experience; it's also been very tough – Mamo mentioned this notion of working an eighty-hour week. I thought I had a tough job in the newspaper. We used to go around telling ourselves things like 'deadlines', 'pressure' and 'the editor is never happy' made life difficult. I found it was nothing compared to looking after three children. It is a job that you take on and I thoroughly enjoy it. I wouldn't swap those twelve years and I still have more to go. I know it was mentioned in the introduction that I have begun to build a practice in psychotherapy, but I am still focused on the home; I still plan around whether I can be at home to do this, that and the other at all times.

In the context of this conference on the family and the family's place in society, I had a sense that once I made the decision to be a stay-at-home dad, I had this funny idea that lots of other men would follow, that I wouldn't be the only guy at the school. However, for ten years of bringing my children to primary school, I was nearly the only man there. There were two men who started out with me by complete coincidence, and by two years later both of them had packed it in and gone back to work, begging for their offices and their desks back. There wasn't the flood of men I expected. There are other men who are involved in all sorts of parenting and that is great to see, but the complete leap into being the primary carer – the cooker, cleaner and shopper – that is still pretty much a rarity. I suppose that's my way of saying that I found the whole business of being at home at first quite isolating. Women will tell you that when they become stay-at-home parents it is quite isolating. So I found that when the women would get together and have coffee mornings and things like that, there is a different dynamic at work when you are a man at home. I found that what I had to do was get involved in everything. I was on the parish committee, I was on the PTA, I was the fundraiser for the new primary school, I edited the parish newsletter, I did my share on sports rosters, playground rosters, swim rosters – anything at all I could get involved in I just simply did. I did it in order to get over the whole isolating thing – that was a very predominant feeling. If I hadn't done these things, I would be at home and the kids would be at school and there is only so much ironing that you can do.

That changed a little bit with secondary school, where by the time my kids had started – they are still in secondary school now, although I have one that has left and she has gone on to third level now – I just couldn't take another PTA meeting. So now they were out of the house even more and I was at home even more and I've always had bits and pieces of work to keep me busy, but nevertheless the business of being the parent at home can still be that it's just you. I suppose that I was applying that way of thinking to the context of this conference, this notion of the family, and as we know from the Constitution it is the basic unit of society. Then I began to think that's all very fine and dandy, but that basic unit of society exists primarily on the strength of the relationships that go into it. We have heard a lot about relationships earlier, and there is a kind of expectation that that is just simply going to happen: there is a governmental expectation and there is a personal expectation. In the place in which I lived in Dublin, the people around me were all very nice and friendly, but I still had that feeling of being on my own to a large extent. I was just wondering how prevalent that is, that the basic unit of society is kind of an isolated unit of society. That its strengths only to a degree come from its internal relationships, much like the honeycomb: that single little cell whose strength also comes from its connections to the outside.

I feel that sometimes when I look back on my twelve years that that part around our unit was a construction that had to be put in place, that it actually wasn't there until I went out and said, 'I'll do that' and 'I'll get involved here' and 'I'll give lifts here and I'll give lifts there'. We hear a lot about the fragmentation of communities; we hear a lot about the fact that people aren't connected as much; the idea that neighbourliness isn't as common as it used to be; the fact that people are independently minded now, which is kind of like saying, 'I'll watch out for myself', and that is all well and good.

Yet, families are trying to operate within this milieu and I feel that this puts a burden on the unit of society, a burden which the unit of society was never intended to carry. I think I have come to the belief that the family unit was always intended to be linked into other family units.

I always remember that as a stay-at-home dad one of the joys is daytime TV, as you all know. I remember watching Oprah Winfrey one day, she had these people on and they were talking about rebuilding communities in the US, and it was very interesting and very inspiring as only Oprah can be. She had this phrase, which she had picked up from Africa somewhere, which went, 'It takes a village to raise a child'. I thought it was a very powerful notion that relationships which exist in the nuclear family in the western model are incredibly intense. As a therapist, I have people coming to me who are suffering from some form of damaged family relationship. While everyone's story is different, the common element is this intensity of experience, which is completely undiluted by access to other primary figures in the broader family, in the extended family or even in the community. You can see it even in small things. You don't see people telling someone else's child anymore to 'Behave yourself' or 'Don't do that' – you just don't. The authority isn't there so it has absolutely no effect. That's just one little example of this notion that I'm talking about, this disconnectedness within the networks that strengthen the family unit. And again, like the good doctor I heard earlier, I deal with couples that are coming in and trying to make a relationship work with enormous burdens – some of them very real, for example, there might be financial problems or a disability, there might be all sorts of things going on. But very often they don't paint in the cultural gaps that exist for all of us, for example, the things I'm talking about, the supports, the invisible supports that we once took for granted in what we used to call our wider community, which just aren't there any more.

That would be my sense coming out of a twelve-year background as a stay-at-home dad. As I said, I have been very lucky to do it, but there were times when I looked at the bank balance on a monthly basis and wondered if I was so lucky to be doing this or not, but I wouldn't swap it for the world. I often wonder whether I should wheel in the kids and find out, 'Well, I found it enriching, what do you think?' They would probably say, 'Go away Dad'.

That's basically my story, I don't have anything else to add, other than that the family is vitally important, it is the last line, it is the last thing we have, it is the place that enriches us, it is the place that we are formed. It is interesting that when I was staying at home in the middle of all of this rhetoric about the family being the unit of society, they brought in individualisation. It is a tax thing where if the spouse went back out to work they would be better off on a tax basis. I couldn't get over this and there was no protest, although I suppose there wouldn't be, but I didn't even really hear any people complaining about this. Even in the pro-family environment, even with it written into the Constitution, these little things can slip in under the radar. I mention that because I was jumping around at the radio when I heard it, but it became history then. As I said, if anyone needs advice on baking, cooking or putting together a three-course meal in twenty minutes – I'm the guy.

Our final panel member for this discussion is Geraldine Reidy. Geraldine is the mother of two grown-up children and she is going to look at things from the perspective of a woman who raised her children alone following the break-up of her marriage twenty-five years ago. Her parenting experience spans more than three decades and two continents, because she spent over twenty years living in North America. Geraldine is also a representative of OPEN, One Parent Groups in Ireland, *and as a trainer in parenting skills, so she has much to bring to this session.*

Family Life Today: The Greatest Revolution?

Geraldine Reidy

I am here today because OPEN has asked me to speak about my experience as the head of a one-parent family. To tell you my story I must first give you some background. I was born on Monday, 17 November 1952 in my grandmother's house in Kings Island, Limerick. Otherwise known in Limerick as 'the Abbey' or 'the Parish'. I am the fourth child in a staunch Irish Catholic family of eleven – well, there were actually twelve children; one of my sisters, Philomena, died when she was six months old. I have two godparents, but I have no idea who they are and my mother doesn't remember. I don't know how anyone could be expected to remember the names of twenty-four couples over a period of twenty-five years and who went with who. By the way, my real name is not Geraldine, my real name is Anne. My older brother, who I have called Kevin for fifty-seven years, is named Thomas. I also have a younger sister called Anne, she is the eighth child in the family. We must have had my poor mother driven demented by the time she got to my sister Anne to make such a mistake. In other words, I was born into a typical Irish family. When I was about three or four years old, the family moved to a new housing estate in Garryowen. My grandmother, my mum's mother, came to live with us. She was a widow and had gone blind a number of years before the move. A lot of our new neighbours were also from the Abbey. I have no recollection of my early years in the Abbey, but from the nostalgic way that my mother, grandmother and the neighbours spoke about it, it was the only place in the country worth living in. My mother and grandmother were both born in the Abbey and so got their grounding from there. Their families lived there for over one hundred years. We lived in Garryowen for five to six years when my parents bought a house back in the Abbey. My children lived in a one-parent family, thousands of miles away from the Abbey, but they in turn got their grounding from me and my stories of the Abbey and Ireland.

Ireland in the 1950s was not very conducive to raising a large family, mostly due to very high unemployment. My parents had very strong work ethics and so my dad, along with many other fathers, headed off to England looking for work. I remember the registered envelopes arriving home every week to my mum. I remember the birthday cards with an English ten shilling note inside arriving for each one of us children as our birthdays came up. Availability of work must have improved, so my dad came home and started work in Limerick dock. With that came the Sunday walks; it didn't matter where we went we just wanted to go along with him. When unemployment rose again he signed up with the Irish shipping lines and was gone again for six to ten months of the year. As children, we never questioned his absence, we knew he was our dad and that he worked on the ships. It didn't seem at all strange to us that he wasn't around all the time like some of the other fathers, and we also lived in the anticipation of the presents we would get from him when he returned home – and they were numerous. My children went to visit their dad one weekend every month and loved going there. They also talked with him on the phone whenever they wanted. It was my husband and I who divorced, not my children and their father.

As in all families there were good times and bad, and as children and teenagers we took everything for granted. As a family, we knelt and said the Rosary every night directly after supper and before we were allowed to go outside to play. In winter it was before we sat down around the fire to hear my grandmother and father tell us ghost stories, while my mother knit our cardigans and jumpers and sewed. As children we learned to knit and sew also. We didn't question our family values. We didn't know such a thing existed – what are they? We did what we were told or otherwise we were known as 'the brazen thing' or 'I'm going to kill you when I get my hands on you'. We didn't give our opinions because the response was, 'Don't talk back'. So we learned to keep our questions and opinions to ourselves and that way we stayed out of trouble, at home anyway. We learned not to tell the whole truth about our whereabouts and other things, and basically this was done out of fear of being murdered when they got their hands on us. In reality, my dad never laid a hand on any of us, although my mum did give us the odd swat.

I grew up, got married, emigrated to Canada and had two children. I had heard stories of parents divorcing and children becoming juvenile delinquents, doing drugs and alcohol. I thought to myself that I could never do that to my children. I wanted the same family life with them as I had growing up. I might add that at that time I did not know any single-parent families myself to dispute any of the stories, and so true to form I didn't question the stories I heard. As a child, I had watched as my mum made all the financial decisions, everything was paid for in cash: the mortgage payment every month, the grocery money put aside, the electricity bills, the coal bills, money put aside for First Communion and Confirmation clothes, for Christmas clothes and toys, and for whichever one of us needed shoes and clothes throughout the year. And thank God for the Parish Credit Union where we could throw in a couple of bob every week for any emergencies that might arise. We learned the value of money and how to manage it. Eventually, my dad got a permanent job in Limerick and stayed home for good.

In Toronto, I listened to single parents being interviewed on television about how little they had to live on. From our cosy positions, my friend and I could not understand why they could not live on what I later realised was a meagre amount. We could manage on that, of course we could, if we had to. But, what we had not factored into the equation was the stress of having to manage it on a week-in, week-out basis, for God knows how many years. After eight and a half years, I left my marriage with my two children; my daughter was six years and five months old and my son was six and a half hours away from being born. The decision to leave was a tough one and had been coming for quite some time. Sticking to the decision was even tougher. It would have been so much easier to go back, but for the wrong reason; that reason being financial. But, here again I was blessed: my income was triple what other single parents were getting on social welfare, and my children and I continued to get private health insurance and dental insurance through my husband's job. Six months into my separation I decided to return to Ireland, as I thought it would be easier to survive there. I would have the support of my family and my children would be in the safe care of my mum while I was at work. Things didn't turn out quite as I had expected. I was unable to secure work on the grounds that I had a young baby and would not show up for work if either one of my children were sick. I put a deposit on a house. It took months for a decision to be made regarding the mortgage, based on the fact that I was now a single parent. The blatant discrimination made me really angry so, consequently, after nine months in Ireland, I high-tailed it back to Canada. This time I went to a small provincial town where I knew an Irish couple with children close to the ages of my own two children. It was difficult finding an apartment because most of the buildings catered for adults only. I finally secured a sub-let for the summer from students in Queens University student housing complex. Now that I had a roof over our heads for the next three months, I had time to search for a permanent home for us. It would have to be in the same area because my daughter was enrolled in the school close by. I heard of an apartment becoming available in the complex in September, the only snag was that you had to be a student at the university to apply for it. So, why not become a mature student? After all, I had always wanted to go to university, now was my chance and I'd secure our living accommodation at the same time. My daughter was in school full time, I could drop her off on my way to university and be home on time to pick her up again. I was eligible for a student loan, so that solved the problem of college fees, but who was going to look after my eighteen-month-old son and could I afford the day-care? Upon further investigation, I discovered the college day-care centre. It turned out that, because I was a single parent, I was entitled to one of the subsidised spots, which were held open specifically for single parents – finally being a single parent had its advantages. I stayed on in college for two years until I could no longer afford to go.

As it turned out, subsidised day-care was the only advantage to being a single parent. Living in a country thousands of miles away from Irish society, I finally started to rebel against some of my Irish upbringing. As a parent, I had made the decision to encourage my children to voice their opinions in a respectful manner and to include them in the decision process; after all they would have to survive in a world totally alien to the sheltered environment I had grown up in. The only problem was that I had not experienced such an open approach to rearing a family and certainly not on my own. Again, I was very fortunate in the sense that a lot of parenting magazines were available to me. I just had to decide which one was the right approach for my family. And, as it happened, most of my new friends were single parents facing the same problems as myself. I no longer felt comfortable in a coupled society, so I muddled through some very good decisions and some really disastrous ones; maybe that goes with the territory of being a parent.

From both my parents I learned a lot of my values: the responsibility of raising a family, how to balance a budget so that we could survive through tough economic times, the importance of God or spirituality in our lives for direction and the value of kindness and empathy. Looking at my children, and talking to my children, I know I have passed those values on to them and have added a few more, such as the value of listening to children and doing something out of respect and not fear. These values have carried us through good times and bad. I am proud of my children and I know that these values will take them through into many varied situations in their own lives. My life's experience as well as their own has enriched their lives no end. Through all these years, I had never realised that my mother was a single parent for the best part of each year, and many other women whose husbands had to go abroad to work were in the same boat, so to speak. They were not single-parent families voluntarily; circumstances dictated their situation. They were not single-parent families because they had split up as a couple; they were single-parent families because they had the Irish Sea and sometimes oceans between them.

So what makes my family different from two-parent families? To me it is just the label that society has plastered on us. My sense of grounding or belonging was based on my parents, and my children's grounding has been based on mine. My children's basic value system is intergenerational, with each generation deleting from and adding to the other. So, in essence, we are just another typical Irish family muddling our way through.

Discussion

Delegate (Department of Social & Family Affairs): With the wealth of experience of the panel, in terms of parenting supports, is there any one thing that you think – in light of today's challenges that parents are facing – that you could recommend that the State could possibly be providing that could help parents?

Kevin: I think childcare would be an interesting place to start. It always strikes me that childcare is a huge problem with people having to work, especially when both parents have to work. Also, the state of some of the primary schools today is a disgrace in post-Celtic Tiger Ireland. And, at a Local Authority level, there is a great lack of facilities, even playgrounds and open spaces for children to play.

We talk about ourselves as a pro-family society; if that was the case the school you want to send your child to should be on the next corner. I know that's an ideal. I was in Sweden recently and that's a system they have, the crèche you send your child to before they go to school is on the other corner, there's always a swimming pool close by where you can take your children at the weekend, there's always a playground, among other things. That is an attitude that a society has taken about itself and about its children.

I'm at a stage where I have teenagers now and – you have heard it before and it's nothing new – they don't have places to go. I thought Michael McDowell's idea of coffee shops was a great idea – I think it was an idea ahead of its time and I hope it comes back because my children, not necessarily in this direct way, are going from alcohol-free discos straight to bars – that's the progression in our society as it seems to me. As regards to the isolation that exists in our nuclear family model, we are like the polar bear on that little bit of ice because of global warming – a big powerful entity on a tiny little space, and that's what I sometimes think of when thinking about the family today.

Geraldine: With regards to services I would very much recommend providing parenting courses for parents. Today, child rearing is very different from what it was when I was growing up, and somewhat different from when my children were growing up. The challenges that are out there for young people in our society, between drugs, alcohol and violence, are just incredible. Unless parents within the home can build the confidence and the self-esteem of their children themselves, to go out into the world and be able to say no and be comfortable and confident in saying no, that is to me one of the most important things that Social Services can now provide to every parent in the country.

Ciana: Are parents interested or open to the idea of doing parenting courses? That's something you actually deliver, but perhaps because parents might come looking for it. What sort of an uptake do you think there would be?

Geraldine: 'Strengthening Families, Strengthening Communities' is the new parenting programme that has been introduced in Ireland by OPEN about a year ago. To date there has been a huge voluntary uptake for the programmes. There are some parents who have been requested by Social Services or the HSE, for example, to attend it, but primarily it is a voluntary attendance programme.

Mamo: Grandparents are quite often involved in the care of their grandchildren; I think many of them are being asked to do it beyond their physical capacity. I did a bit of research some years ago and I discovered one grandmother who was looking after three lively boys, and there was a fast flowing river at the back of her house and a busy road at the front of it. She had a heart bypass and suffered from arthritis and I didn't think it was even safe for the children to be there. Other stories like that which I heard lead me to wonder about having day-care centres that would provide support for grandparents looking after children if they have to do it; a place where the grandparents could take them where they would have the support of others and it would be a safe environment.

Delegate (Corrib Lions Club, Galway): I am a dad with four children ranging from ages five to ten years old. Based on your own life experiences, what advice would you give a guy like me and my wife. What would be your top tip?

Mamo: I think time. It is very hard to do in today's busy, busy world, but I think quality time spent with the children and doing things with them which they will remember later on is important. I still remember my father on every Good Friday (we lived in Kilfinnan, Co. Limerick) would take us for a walk through the Ballyhoura Hills, and there was a place there where we would sit in among the rocks and he would tell us the story of Androcles and the Lion. This became a tradition every Good Friday. I remember that and other little things like that, so I would say giving them your time is the best gift you could give them.

Geraldine: I would have to agree with Mamo, but would also add that you should listen very carefully to what your children are saying to you.

Kevin: I always think it's a good idea to make them laugh and have fun with them. We can become very po-faced and serious, intense and burdened by our own things. What I found, and it took me a lot of time to learn, was to just park that somewhere and try and have some fun with them.

Mamo: I think too that television should be banned at meal times. Too many families have the television on when they are having their meals. They should have one family meal in the day where they all sit down together and settle the world.

All my family are married, only one broken marriage among them (my son has custody of his two boys), and they could sort the whole world out because they had this intense discussion at every meal, the dialogue between them was amazing. I also have to say that a few of the boys have done the parenting at home that Kevin talked about, and one of the boys used to leave his children off in the morning and the women would be there chatting and he would say, 'I'd love to stay and chat ladies but I have a pile of ironing waiting for me'.

Kevin: I agree with Mamo, except you'll miss *Home and Away!*

Delegate (Director of 'One Family'): I am delighted that the panel have started to open up in our discussion today on what family is in Ireland, because 'One Family' has been working for thirty-six years with people who have been parenting on their own and increasingly with people who are sharing parenting. I think a lot of the discussions that I heard today were really about one type of family and that is the family based on marriage. So it's very good that we have started to begin to think about the fact that there are many, many other types of families. The reason I'm asking this is that one of the big challenges that many of the families we work with face is the fact that they find it very difficult to perceive themselves as a family; they often don't think that they are a real family and that is often due to the very negative messages they are getting from the wider society. That leads to a decrease in self-confidence and self-esteem in their family, which we see have negative impacts on their children. I wonder if the panel would like to respond in general or specifically about one-parent families and about negative messages, and I suppose what responsibilities the rest of us can take to ensure that that doesn't happen.

Ciana: Geraldine, you might kick off with that – this is something you experienced when you came back to Ireland originally and when your children were very small. Then you returned to Canada and now you have been back here again for twelve years, so you have a huge range of experience where this is concerned.

Geraldine: I suppose I had more guts than brains when I started out as a single-parent family. From my own circumstances I was very angry when I started out and I think anger can move mountains. I was brought up in a society where shame played a huge part – you kept everything from the neighbours and you didn't tell them anything, you would hide this and hide that in shame. I was three months separated before I even told my parents about it, and I wouldn't have even told them at that point only for the fact that my mum phoned up and said she was coming over to visit for a holiday, so I had no choice. I didn't tell her then, I hung up the phone, phoned my sister and I said, 'Now you go in and tell Mum that I'm separated'.

But I had to adapt, something clicked in my mind: my children and I were just as valuable as other two-parent families out there. We were valuable as a two-parent family when there were four of us, so are we less valuable now that there are only three? What if I were a widow? I would still be in a single-parent family; if my husband was in jail I would be a single-parent family; if my husband worked abroad I would be a single-parent family, so what was the difference between me separating and divorcing? I was in a 'dysfunctional family', my children were living in a broken home and these ideas and these words and directions towards us really made me even angrier, and I thought, to heck with it. We are what we are and I suppose I was an independent person growing up too, and my family gave us that sense even though we were in a sheltered family unit – a staunch Irish Catholic sheltered family unit. We were brought up to be independent while sharing an interdependence in the family. I think I kicked back to that, my independence: this is who I am, this is who we are, I'm not ashamed of my position in life, I'm not ashamed of having my two children, even though they now, in society's eyes, no longer have a father. They had a father just like I had a father, who through necessity had to work abroad, and I think I fell back on all those experiences.

I took my strength from the fact that I had two very strong women who were role models in my life. My mother raising eleven children most of the time on her own – and it was my mother who raised us, and within our communities it was the women who raised their family. That was what it was like at that time in Irish society, it was the life we knew in Irish society. That wasn't to demean any of the fathers: they were either working abroad to support their family or they were gone all day; they came home in the evening and they were either tired and went to bed or went out to the pub for a drink at nine or ten o'clock. It was the mothers who carried the burden of raising these large families. So I suppose I have a lot to be grateful for in having my mother and my grandmother, because I was able to fall back on their experience and just get on with my life. It was tough at times – it was very, very tough – and it was tough to carry the stigma of being a single parent, but you have to have the right attitude. I had very supportive friends as well while I was abroad, who were more like extended family, and my children were treated as equals.

Therefore, until we actually get out there and stand up and say, we are not broken families, we may be different from what our Constitution recognises the family as being, but we are not broken and we are not dysfunctional. I am extremely proud of my children, I am very proud of lots of other children from single-parent families that are no different from two-parent families. You need to get up there as an individual and stand up for your rights as a single parent and as a single-parent family.

Ciana: Mamo, in a sense you also were a lone parent for quite a long period.

Mamo: That's right, and I never anticipated that I would be. It happened so suddenly. I suppose when you have had a shoulder to cry on, not having a shoulder to cry on is devastating. Although, I have to say that when living in a rural Irish town the community closes in around you. I had amazing support from friends and neighbours and from the women in the ICA. It was they who convinced me to come out again. I didn't want to go anywhere, I didn't want to leave the house, and through my membership of the ICA I had a second family around me, as it were, and that was wonderful. So belong to something, have something that is outside of your life with your husband or wife, have a circle of friends, I think that is hugely important. The other thing I did was start to write a diary just a year before Eugene died, and that became the shoulder I cried on. I wrote down what I was feeling and I have been writing it ever since. I have often advised people who suddenly find themselves alone to write down how you are feeling, because people get bored with you loading your problems on them; but there is still a way of doing it, because sometimes by writing it down you can let it go.

Kevin: I think the stigma attached to single-parent families is an extra burden that is unnecessary to carry. I think it's a pity that we are still talking about a stigma attached to single-parent families in this day and age. I work with some pretty dysfunctional people who come from two-parent families. So this notion that it is a wrong way or a right way is part of thinking that, in personal terms, belongs to another time, as far as I can see.

Delegate: I can identify greatly with Mamo McDonald. I'm a mother of twelve children and a grandmother of twenty-four and also I lost my husband in similar circumstances, which meant I was left in the position you have already outlined. As a mother with a young child still at school you are not prepared for this. You haven't been prepared, first of all, for a large family and, secondly, you haven't been prepared for being alone. Just one thing which I can't understand with regards to the State is that it costs a lot for child-minding. Now the childminder in Ireland, whether they are male or female, is not considered to be a labour unit, so, therefore, they don't have any monetary value or any rights to such things as pensions. So the monetary stress, allied to all the others, is unbelievable. I'm surprised that, as women, we don't look to have women who work in the home granted self-employment status or, as Kevin said, he was working in the home but it didn't have a monetary value. I think its something which we have to look for. Thank you so much for your contribution, it's just wonderful to hear from people we call survivors.

Ciana: I suspect that Kevin would probably consider that, not alone are people who parent full-time in the home not supported financially, but in fact, as you described earlier as what is called individualisation, you'll probably respond that they are 'penalised', as you say.

Kevin: It was a small but cutting move by the government at the time. I think the bigger point is, as Mamo touched on, the notion of working an eighty-hour week, which is probably the average for parents. This morning, before I came down here, I had one child coming back from a school trip and her room had been unused for two weeks, so I was running around her room this morning at seven with the 'Mr Sheen' to get rid of the dust, to give it a bit of a tidy up for her before she comes home. There are other things like coming in on an evening after doing other bits and pieces and sorting laundry until eleven or twelve at night, or whatever it might be. That is all part of what you're talking about, there's that continuous thing. I'm not complaining about this, but what I'm saying is that this is a fact, and if parents were to be supported, whether they are lone-parents or not, for providing the work that cements this unit of society, whatever the model is, that is enshrined in our Constitution, if we got Mamo on it and if she did a job like she did with the elderly at the protests recently, I'm sure we might see a change but it would cost an absolute fortune.

Mamo: In Germany they have it well done: for every child you have you are entitled to three years' worth of stamps, as it were, for a pension, you get three years' pension rights for every child you rear. I think that's a good thing.

Ciana: I think if the Department of Social Welfare are listening, that is another practical tip. On that note, we have to draw to a close. I have to say a heartfelt thanks to Mamo, Kevin and Geraldine for sharing so generously of their own experiences, be that within the home, but also their wider experiences, their connections with different organisations and for giving their time today. Thank you also to the delegates for your contributions and questions, it was an absolute pleasure to be in your company.

Where Does Family Fit?

Implications of the New Economic Reality for Family Life

Jim Power
Chief Economist with Friends First,
Lecturer at Dublin City University and Michael Smurfit
Graduate School of Business

I was asked to examine what is happening to the Irish economy at the moment and the implications it might have for family life in Ireland. I stress that I am an economist rather than a sociologist, so please bear with me in relation to some of the observations I will be making about the societal impact of what has happened in our economy. Specifically, I want to talk a little bit about the whole legacy of the Celtic Tiger. I then want to consider where the Irish economy is today and what the future might hold. I then want to identify what I would regard as some of the significant economic and social challenges now facing Ireland and the possible implications for family life.

First of all, I will outline some of the characteristics of Ireland today. I have been a pretty vocal critic of much of what has happened in this country over the past decade. I have been concerned about the fact that there has been much more emphasis on the quantity rather than quality of growth. In other words, I believe that there has been a huge push for economic growth at all costs. Economic growth has been regarded as the be all and end all and, unfortunately, there has been a lot less focus on the quality of that economic growth. Indeed, in many aspects of Ireland's social and economic development in recent years quality has been sacrificed for quantity.

Family Life Today: The Greatest Revolution?

The following are some of the characteristics of Ireland that have developed over the past decade and which are still very obvious today:

- **Significant wealth creation** has occurred in the economy over the last ten years, there is no doubt about that. I mean wealth in terms of large and numerous cars, property, the ability to go on three or four foreign holidays a year and so on.
- There has been a total **preoccupation with property**. I have been absolutely astounded over the years by the number of Irish people who have invested in foreign properties overseas, who have become experts on the Bulgarian property market or the Cape Verdian property market. I suppose my gauge for this is that every Sunday, one of the first things I have done over the years is look at the property supplement in the *Sunday Business Post* to see what the latest property hotspot is. The notion of Irish people going to places like Venezuela, India, Cape Verde and many more locations besides to invest in property astounded me. I think we are definitely preoccupied with property, there is no doubt about that. I know a number of farmers from where I come from in Waterford who are major property holders in Berlin at the moment. It is astounding.
- The **commuter belt has been re-defined** due to lack of proper planning. I leave Dublin at 5:30 a.m. quite frequently, and it always depresses me to see the stream of traffic coming into Dublin at that hour of the morning from all approach routes. It really struck me very forcefully a couple of years ago by something I observed. I was coming up to Baggot Street Bridge on my bike at 6:30 a.m. and observed beside me a young couple in the front of a car and a baby asleep in the back seat. This is no way to live. The whole

notion of people having to commute for hours to and from work is quite extraordinary and depressing, but in many cases there is no choice. It will also be interesting to observe the social impact of a generation delivered to and collected from crèches at all hours of the day and night.

- **Substance abuse** is obviously a significant issue in Ireland today. I am not sure if that is something new in the Irish psyche, I suspect we always had a predisposition towards substance abuse, but over the past decade we have been able to afford more – so we do it more.

- There has been a significant **deterioration in diet** due to more frantic lifestyles and this has given rise to a serious issue with obesity, which is putting a strain on the health service.

- The **quality of public services** has deteriorated and in many ways it is clear that the economy has totally outgrown its public services and public infrastructure. Unfortunately, nobody had the vision to prioritise these areas and we are all poorer as a result.

I would like to pose a question, and it is the question I'm trying to answer today: are we happier as a nation than we were ten or fifteen years ago? Some are, but many certainly are not. Generally, I think that whilst there have been a lot of positive developments in recent years, there have also been a lot of developments that I certainly would have significant reservations about.

In relation to this whole issue about the quality of Irish life today, a key question to answer is if family life is *better*? It is in some ways and it certainly is not in other ways, which I will try to explain.

The Celtic Tiger was a period of remarkable economic growth; we saw a doubling of employment over a ten-year period from just over a million people to about 2.2 million people in employment today. Perhaps one of the biggest changes of all has been the turn around in migratory flows. In the last decade we have seen strong inward migration into the country. In many ways that was very positive because a lot of the Irish that were forced to emigrate during the 1980s came back in the 1990s and the 2000s. We have also seen a lot of non-Irish come into the country and become part of the Irish economy, if not Irish society.

We have gone on a massive and absolutely dramatic borrowing and spending binge over the last decade. We have seen a massive escalation of house prices at least up to as late as twelve months ago. As I said, there has been a total obsession with property investment and development; so many people around the country have become property investors and property developers. There has been a dramatic change in the standard of living in the country, and I suppose more importantly there has been a dramatic change in peoples' expectations. To me this represents one huge challenge for many people. When I graduated from college in the 1980s, the reality was that the majority of the brightest and the best left the country to get meaningful employment and the rest of us stayed behind. As we evolved into the 1990s and 2000s, the whole situation changed dramatically. For people graduating from college or even from secondary school it became a sellers' market – you could name your price: this is the job I want; this is how much I want to be paid. Therefore, expectations adjusted absolutely enormously and people's expectations now in terms of material goods and material services are very high – we all now expect three or four foreign holidays per annum, flat screen TVs and the latest car model. Our standard of living and our expectations have changed dramatically, but they are going to have to change back again because the reality is now starting to look quite a bit different.

Implications of the New Economic Reality for Family Life

The Irish economy is now in serious difficulty and the challenges presenting themselves are immense. There is a lot of personal debt out there; we have seen totally irrational growth in house prices; and we have developed a completely inordinate dependence on property and construction. I have got a lot of things wrong over the years in this world of economics and finance, but three years ago I brought out a report (it wasn't rocket science, believe me) arguing that as an economy we had become inordinately dependent on housing and housing activity, and that we had become like a bird flying on one wing and if anything ever went wrong with that wing, namely construction, we would be in serious trouble. Clearly in the last twelve months something has gone wrong and we are in serious trouble. The big mistake was that policy makers just threw so many of our economic and financial resources into property development at the cost of everything else. One of the things that really depresses me at this stage is that if we couldn't sort out problematical areas like health and education during ten years of incredible wealth creation, what chance have we of actually tackling those problems in a much more modest growth environment going forward? Indeed, an element of the budget that I found utterly depressing and disillusioning was the attempt to claw back funding in areas like education. It is worrying and short-sighted, there is no doubt about that.

Some of our behaviour has been very strange during the Celtic Tiger years. I was on The Marian Finucane Show with Rachael English in January 2008. One of the stories in the paper that morning was that Bus Eireann had launched an IKEA bus service – bussing people from Dublin to IKEA in Northern Ireland every day – while at the same time the bus service in many parts of the country is dire. In my opinion, developments such as this indicate that 'the lunatics have taken over the asylum!'

Family Life Today: The Greatest Revolution?

We have definitely created much, much different expectations and a lot of those expectations, unfortunately or fortunately depending on your perspective, are now starting to look very unreal.

In terms of personal debt, in absolute terms we have basically gone from just over €20 billion back in 1999 to over €140 billion by 2007. The numbers aside, seeing that sort of increase in such a short period of time is extraordinary stuff. Expressed as a percentage of GNP the story is similar, we have gone from 40% to over 90%. That is by any stretch of the imagination one hell of a borrowing binge. That is one of the big legacies we have left from the Celtic Tiger period, and it is definitely one of the strangleholds that is going to have a significant influence on economic and social life in this country over the coming years.

In terms of house prices, we have also experienced pretty mad stuff in many ways – you have seen the average house price go from around €60k in the mid-nineties to over €350k at present. I suppose the good news is that it is now going into reverse, and over the next three or four years I assure you that graph will be heading in a downward direction, which is extremely positive, because it will allow our children the opportunity to afford a house again.

An examination of the cost of living increases in recent years is also interesting, as financial pressure tends to put a lot of pressure on family life. Since the beginning of 2000, the overall cost of living increased by 41.5%. Food prices increased by just 26%, so food price inflation, despite what we were led to believe by Eddie Hobbs and others during the ill-informed debate on the Grocery Order, hasn't been quite as dramatic as in other parts of the economy. Childcare costs have increased by almost 74%, health by 72% and education by 71% – despite the fact that we are meant to have free education. Clothing and footwear prices have fallen as a result of globalisation.

Electricity prices increased by 91% and Local Authority charges by 257%. The bottom line is that over the last eight years the cost of living for families has increased dramatically. Despite the fact we are all earning higher wages and that we have more material wealth, in terms of our disposable incomes there hasn't been that much improvement over the period.

In terms of migration, I would certainly regard the last ten years as an extremely positive development, because I think socially and economically being forced to export your brightest and best and the rest is certainly not the way to go – it is not positive. Voluntary emigration is a good idea, but involuntary emigration is absolutely disastrous economically and socially, and from the point of view of family life.

Enough has been said about where we have come from and what we have created over the last ten years – the facts are the facts, I don't see glasses as half empty or half full, I see the glass as it is and the glass as it is in an Irish context is now very difficult. The economy is in recession, economic growth is contracting, the consumer has slowed sharply as the driver of the economy, the construction contribution has fallen dramatically, the export side of the economy is under serious pressure and the labour market is deteriorating rapidly. In the last twelve months there has been an increase of almost 80,000 in the number of people signing on the dole; that is the largest ever annual increase we have seen in unemployment in this country. The public finances as we know are absolutely dreadful by any definition, and this year and next year we are looking at growth contracting for the first time since the early 1980s.

Undoubtedly, the big story on the Irish economy is the housing adjustment. Back in 2006 we built 93,000 houses. That same year in the UK, with more than ten times our population, they built 180,000 houses. So we were building over half the number of houses they were in the UK with less than one-tenth of the population. So for anyone who doubts the fact, we really, really went overboard with irrational house building in recent years, which created a huge economic and financial dependence and posed a huge vulnerability when it went into reverse. Statistically, we know that for every 10,000 houses less we build it knocks 1% off economic growth. Next year we are going to build about 25,000 houses, so there has been a decline of more than 70,000 over a three-year period, which translates into about 7% off economic growth. Thus, the Irish economic story is a housing story – that is where the real pain is being driven – but unfortunately, a lot like the Waterford hurling team at that funeral in Croke Park in early September 2008, anything that could go wrong has gone wrong for the Irish economy over the last twelve months. The whole sub-prime crisis and the financial problems it has created has seriously exasperated the Irish economic situation. Regardless of what politicians in government will tell you, the Irish economy today is in a very, very perilous state of health, and I think that anybody who believes otherwise is naïve. It astounded me that up until relatively recently there was a total unwillingness to have any rational debate on the Irish economy. Anyone that dared express a negative view was described as a merchant of doom and gloom by the former Taoiseach, by his successor and by a lot of others. In this light, it was quite amazing when members of Fianna Fáil came out of the think-tank in Galway in September 2008 and suddenly started telling us that 'the country is in a bad state'. What they were trying to do was condition us for the budget, which was to come in October. So it is all about managing expectations. I am totally and utterly cynical about the political process and the manner in which it has influenced the way the economy has developed over the last ten years. I will go back to the point I made earlier on, and I am going to make it a number of times before I eventually finish: we have put way too much emphasis on quantity and not enough on quality.

Implications of the New Economic Reality for Family Life

Looking at the labour market situation, because from the point of view of any family, but particularly a family that has taken on a high level of debt, which most families have in recent times, a deterioration in the labour market represents a seriously negative development. We have seen in the last year an absolutely rapid and massive deterioration in the labour market. The number of people signing on the live register increased by almost 80,000, and in terms of employment we saw that during the second quarter of 2008, employment actually fell by over 26,000, which is the first time we have seen that situation develop for a long time. Unfortunately, if I go down through every single sector of the Irish economy – financial services, manufacturing, construction, the retail sector and the public sector – it is very difficult to see any of those sectors creating employment in this economy over the next twelve months at least. In fact, all of those sectors will be shedding employment.

That is the social reality of what is happening to our economy at the moment. The number of people signing on the live register is rising strongly and could hit 400,000 by the end of 2009, and many more jobs will be lost across the economy over the next twelve months. That is a fairly dire outlook for the labour market and it is one that has huge implications for family life and family finances in this country.

Politicians of the government variety would argue that relative to where we were in the 1980s, we are in a very strong position – the unemployment rate is at 6.1% of the labour force compared to 16–18% back in the 1980s. There is truth in that, but the point is, and I think this is a very important point, the trend is more important than the level. When we had 16–18% unemployment we had an appropriate level of debt, we had an appropriate level of economic and financial expectation, whereas when we went into a situation of full employment we adjusted our lifestyles accordingly – debt levels increased and our expectations changed, so when you start to see the labour market deteriorating, those expectations become unattainable.

Looking at where the jobs are and are not being created in the economy over the last twelve months, as a farmer from Waterford I am delighted to see agriculture back in business again. Agriculture and many rural economies, in my view, were victims rather than beneficiaries of the Celtic Tiger period, because agriculture had to compete with construction, for example, for labour and couldn't do so. I found that over the last decade farming and agricultural communities became utterly dispirited; they were being left behind by the Celtic Tiger and construction was the only place to be in the economy. It is good to see that situation turning around.

The worrying thing about that labour market situation is that most of the jobs that have been created in this economy in the last five or six years have been in construction, the public sector and, to a slightly lesser extent, in retail. Those three sectors will not be job creators over the next couple of years, so it creates a difficult labour market outlook. There has been way too much focus on the quantity of jobs created rather than the quality and sustainability of those jobs. We are now paying a high price for this approach.

There are now many pressures on Irish consumers, and we are all consumers to some extent. Consumer spending and consumer confidence have weakened dramatically in the last twelve to eighteen months. The reasons are fairly obvious, and these are the pressures that are bearing down on all of us as individual consumers.

Interest rates: up until very recently interest rates had more than doubled over the previous three years. Thankfully, that is changing and will continue to change, but the doubling of interest rates we saw from December 2005 up until July 2008 imposed a lot of financial pressure on heavily indebted people.

Falling house prices: if you were lucky enough to have got on the housing ladder over the last decade, as house prices increased you became wealthier on paper. This encouraged us to borrow and to spend, creating what economists would call 'a positive consumer wealth effect'. That is now going into reverse with house prices falling dramatically, and I believe that between the peak of the market in 2006 and the trough of the market some time in 2009, prices will have adjusted by between 40–50% in a downward direction. That does represent a massive destruction of wealth, and for people who have borrowed and spent on the back of that housing wealth it creates a vulnerability. The positive thing, and it is a big positive, is that for people who are not on the housing ladder an opportunity to do so is now presenting itself. Therefore, I would unambiguously argue that the decline we are seeing in house prices is extremely positive from an economic and a societal point of view.

Collapsing Irish equity market: the Irish equity market has lost 80% of its value in the last twelve months. For anybody holding shares that represents a nightmare situation, but is even more serious for people who have pensions. Pensions unfortunately hold about 70% in equities, not all in the Irish equity market thankfully, but the equity wealth destruction we have seen has put serious pressure on people's pensions, which poses challenges.

Increase in the cost of living: this has had a huge impact on people. The good news is that over the next couple of years inflation is set to fall rapidly – food prices, oil prices and interest rates decreasing will take inflation down.

The fiscal background: the public finances have deteriorated so rapidly it is extraordinary, and I am not being political about this, that we are now paying the price for total mismanagement of the public finances over the last seven or eight years. At the end of the day, during periods of economic boom, allowing spending to grow by 10–12% per annum is absolutely criminal, and the reason why this money was spent was simply because we had it. There was no notion whatsoever that eventually tax revenues would dry up when the housing market went into reverse, there was just a willingness to go on and spend, spend, spend, with no focus whatsoever on the quality of that spending. Look at some of the money that has been spent around the country over the last decade, the situation with deserted villages in Leitrim is a good example. In Kilmacthomas, the village close to where I come from in Waterford, there is a big, ugly apartment block in the middle of the village. At the first Céifin Conference at which I spoke, I mentioned that famous apartment block, and at that stage I would have said there was a sign up saying 'the last few remaining'; today, the last few are still remaining, one is occupied and that is the same story in many parts of rural Ireland. The reason that apartment block was built was because of tax incentives. If you consider the whole misallocation of resources in the economy over the last decade it is quite frightening. Now, when things go into reverse, when the housing bubble ends, where do they start to claw back money?: the medical card fiasco, the cut backs in primary education and the 1% income levy. It is very depressing and very disillusioning stuff, and it is going to get worse over the next couple of years – there is no doubt about that.

Credit growth: there has been a dramatic slow down in credit growth over the past couple of years. At the peak of that credit cycle in 2006 the stock of lending in the economy was growing by 30% per annum; that is a crazy figure, it is totally unsustainable and it has created a huge economic and financial vulnerability for people.

The economic future is difficult. The growth drives of the Celtic Tiger are under pressure because the days of multinationals coming to country towns and creating a thousand jobs are gone. Globalisation is now the biggest challenge for the Irish economy, we are competing with the Chinese, the Indian and the Eastern European economies of this world; they are much cheaper and they are also investing a lot more money in education than we are at this juncture. So it is going to be extremely difficult for Ireland to compete on the multinational stage, and when you hear the soundings and indeed some of the events coming out of companies like Dell in Limerick, it highlights the challenge for many rural economies from the pressure on the multinational sector. The excesses of recent years certainly created vulnerability in terms of debt levels. As we move into a different economic environment we are going to have to have a lot more focus on the quality rather than the quantity of what we are doing.

One of the big challenges for society and the economy over the coming years is going to be the balance between taxation and spending. The point is that our expectations have justifiably increased and we now expect first-class infrastructure, first-class education, first-class health and first-class social services. We are not getting them because we are not prepared to pay the level of taxation required to deliver them, and the money we are spending is in many cases not being spent in a prudent way. Increasingly we are going to hear a lot of debate about this balance between taxation and spending. I think it is inevitable that the tax base is going to have to be broadened, and while this will be politically unpopular, the reality is that if we want to sustain public spending in a more difficult economic environment, there is going to have to be a radical adjustment to the taxation system. If we want quality public services:

i)   we are going to have to pay for them and,
ii) we are going to have to have a political commitment that value for money will be achieved from the money that is being spent.

We will have to deal with rising unemployment and that will inevitably raise the horrible spectre of forced emigration again. We are also dealing with a serious negative equity situation. I estimate that there are around 150,000 mortgage holders out there, the value of whose property is less than the value of the mortgage, and that figure is going to increase. If you have a job and you are able to pay your mortgage it is not a huge issue – it is uncomfortable and a situation you don't want to be in, but it is not a huge issue. However, it does become a huge issue if you lose your job, because not alone can you not pay your mortgage, but the value of the house upon which the mortgage is based is less than the mortgage itself, so you are in a serious financial quandary. It happened in the UK in the late 1980s and it took a decade to get out of it.

The excesses and the binge culture that has evolved in Ireland in recent years have certainly created a huge vulnerability. Furthermore, the regional economic development model has not delivered. Economic activity is still concentrated in the greater Dublin area, and as you drive around rural Ireland you see more and more rural villages and towns being denuded of people and economic activity. This is quite a sad situation – I thought it was improving for a couple of years, but I think that it has gone back into reverse again.

The pension issue, which I have already mentioned, is a serious one. For many people there is now the very real possiblity of worrying that when they retire, will they have an adequate pension, or will we have a new species in the Irish society called the 'retiring poor'? That is certainly a very real risk.

I return to the point of quality versus quantity and how we can address that. The perceptions of Ireland today are not good. While lifestyles have changed, the economy has outgrown its infrastructure, public services are under serious pressure and crime and substance abuse are all pervasive. Has the individualisation of the tax system worked? In my view, it has not. I am curious about the impact on a generation that has been brought up in a crèche due to this tax policy and about the social implications of that (I have seen some recent mental health research that certainly does worry me). I pose the question: has the quality of life improved? It has in some ways, but certainly not in other ways.

So what are the implications of the new economic reality for the family? There is no doubt that over the last ten or fifteen years the pressure on family life has come under serious strain as expectations soared. I remember my eldest boy, who is now fourteen but was eight at the time, coming home from school after his first day back after the Christmas holidays, he was in a dreadful state because he was the only boy in his class that hadn't got a mobile phone for Christmas. He got one only very recently. It is indicative of the type of peer pressure that has grown up around the whole Celtic Tiger period. The changed economic environment will certainly bring very different challenges, the two biggest challenges being greater financial pressure and greater employment uncertainty. It will also raise the spectre of forced emigration and what that may do for family life.

On the positive side, the level of house prices we have attained in the economy are much more affordable, and the ability of people to get on the housing ladder without taking on a mortgage that will cripple them for thirty or forty years is a major plus. The end of the borrowing binge is certainly also very desirable. Unfortunately, we have an existing stock of debt out there that we are going to have to manage our way through. Thankfully, the rate at which we are taking on that debt is starting to slow down dramatically.

My final point would be that this changed economic reality, while it will bring a lot of pressures, should hopefully bring a much greater sense of reality and sanity back into the equation, and I think that is not before time.

Family Life Today: The Greatest Revolution?

What can we do to engage, address or ease these pressures? Coming at this from a very economic perspective, it is clear that people certainly need to refocus on personal financial planning and budgeting; getting debt levels down is absolutely essential. People need to change their spending behaviour. We will need to prioritise our requirement, which is something that many of us have not had to do in recent years. I think it is essential that we need to start ignoring the Jones's. We certainly need to adjust our expectations to new economic and financial realities. Above all else, we need to keep an incredibly strong focus on education as a society. What I see are cut-backs in education. I am on a Board of Management in a primary and secondary school and I teach in two third-level institutions, and it strikes me that investment in education at all of those levels has been lagging seriously in recent years. If Ireland is to re-emerge from the current economic situation intact, it is the quality of people that will determine our success or failure. That is why I think the focus on the quality of education is absolutely essential. Society is obviously significantly more important than an economy, but I think you would have to recognise and accept that a well-managed, sane economy is essential for a society. A society needs an economy, an economy needs a society; the two are not mutually exclusive.

There are two final points I would like to make. First, we need to distinguish between economic activity and economic welfare. Welfare is a measure of well-being and happiness; economic activity is a financial measure that tells us nothing about the quality of life. Therefore, I do think that we need to focus more on quality of life than on quantity of economic growth.

Finally, I will leave you with a quote from Robert F. Kennedy. In the context of where Ireland has come from in the past decade, this really says it all for me:

> The Gross National Product does not allow for the health of our children, the quality of their education or the joy of their play. It does not include the beauty of our poetry or the strength of our marriages; the intelligence of our public debate, or the integrity of our public officials.

After the ten or fifteen years of the Celtic Tiger, I think we have made a lot of mistakes – we have created significant pressures on family life. However, I do think that we may now be moving back into a sphere where there is going to be a much greater focus on community, society and quality of life, rather than the quantity of economic growth.

The Family in Irish Law

Geoffrey Shannon
Solicitor and Senior Lecturer in Family and Child Law at the
Law Society of Ireland

The question 'What is the meaning of "family"?' is one easily posited, but difficult to answer. A literal interpretation does not do justice to the considerable ideological and conceptual issues involved. The family is a unit in society wherein various interdependent relationships exist. It is a unit concerned with safeguarding the general interests of all concerned, rather than those of any given individual member. In the past, James Connolly described the family as a place where the strongest and most able look after the needs of the weakest and most vulnerable members, as if those needs were the stronger person's own. Selflessness and altruism are traits which ring true within the ideological concept that is the family. There are a number of key characteristics often postulated in relation to what constitutes a family, including commitment, sacrifice, caring for others without monetary compensation, putting the needs of others above your own and supporting each other, both in good times and in bad. In an age when the concerns of the individual, as opposed to the common good, tend to occupy the minds of many, the family and the above mentioned characteristics remain core values upon which society operates. Irrespective of the changing times we live in, the family is a constant feature in society espousing positive ideals. Susan Gary comments on this, stating:

What remains constant is the function families perform for their members and for society. Families create caring, nurturing and loving relationships that do not depend on formal requirements that the family members be related by blood, legal marriage or adoption.[1]

Marriage in Ireland

There has long been a very traditional view of marriage in Ireland. It is often associated with roles: upon marriage the man becomes the breadwinner and the woman the homemaker. This traditional model of marriage was based upon the fact that marriage was a life-long union. The Constitution seeks to safeguard the institution of marriage and protect it from attack. As an institution and class of relationship, marriage is often viewed as being at the pinnacle of social and cultural ideals. Herman Hill Kay has commented that, even those who 'resist the regimentation that marriage entails … accept it as a sort of "gold standard" that signifies the desire for deep and permanent commitment.'[2]

As already noted, marriage is the basis upon which the constitutional family comes into effect. In this regard, various other forms of relationships do not enjoy the benefit of constitutional family rights. In the seminal case of *State (Nicolaou) v. An Bord Uchtála*,[3] Walsh J. stated:

> It is quite clear from the provisions of Article 41, and in particular section 3 thereof, that the family referred to in this Article is the family which is founded on the institution of marriage and, in the context of the Article, marriage means valid marriage under the law for the time being in force in the State. While it is quite true that unmarried persons cohabiting together and the

children of their union may often be referred to as a family and have many, if not all, of the outward appearances of a family, and may indeed for the purposes of a particular law be regarded as such, nevertheless so far as Article 41 is concerned the guarantees therein contained are confined to families based upon marriage.

In *O'B. v. S.*[4] a constitutional challenge was brought in respect of sections 66 and 69 of the Succession Act 1965, which precluded non-marital children from claiming against the intestate estate of a deceased parent. In rejecting the application, the Supreme Court stated:

It has been argued in the present case that the State's special duty of protecting the institution of marriage can be a justification for ensuring that, on intestate succession, children born to either one of the married couple outside the marriage will not succeed on intestacy and that children born of the marriage will so succeed. Thus, it is claimed, the family patrimony will be kept within the family on intestacy, and it is submitted that this is a reasonable and valid means open to the Oireachtas to adopt within the Constitution, if it considers it necessary to do so. Thus the State ensures that the family based on marriage is maintained in a position superior to that of an unmarried union, and thereby honours its guarantee under Article 41, s 1, sub-s 2, of the Constitution. It is not claimed in the present case that there are any particular limitations placed upon the ability of the Oireachtas by legislation to allow intestate succession by children to their parents when the children are born outside marriage, and this Court is not called upon to express any opinion at this time on what limitations may exist in respect of any such legislative ability.

Therefore, it is clear that the Constitution obliges the State to afford special protection to the institution of marriage upon which the family is grounded. Such protection necessitates that other forms of relationships are deprived from the receipt of such rights and entitlements. In the case of *Ennis v. Butterly*[5] an application was brought seeking to enforce the terms of a cohabitation agreement between a non-marital couple. Kelly J. rejected the application as such an agreement sought to provide rights and entitlements commonly reserved for marriage to a non-marital couple. In effect, what was sought was a replication of the advantages of marriage without, in fact, entering into the institution itself. To allow such an application would undermine the institution of marriage and as such it would be contrary to public policy.

In 1995, the family and the institution of marriage underwent a seismic alteration. The introduction of divorce by way of constitutional referendum redefined marriage. In the eyes of the law marriage is no longer 'till death do us part'. The perpetual element that once formed the defining characteristic of marriage no longer exists. Rather, either party to a marriage now enjoys a constitutional right to terminate that marriage, even in the absence of fault on the part of either party. This point is worthy of closer scrutiny. The distinguishing feature that separated marriage from other forms of relationships was its perpetual nature, and it was this feature that justified the superior position afforded to marriage. However, this is no longer the case, and the question now arises as to whether it is now constitutionally permissible to discriminate against other forms of relationships. Why should a marriage that merely lasts for five years prior to divorce be afforded greater status, privileges and rights in comparison to a committed non-marital cohabiting relationship in existence for some ten years or more? Clearly, the non-marital relationship bears more of the hallmarks of the type of relationship which the Constitution sought to protect, as opposed to a short marriage terminated by divorce. Equally, why should a person who has previously terminated a marriage by way of divorce and remarried be afforded these rights and entitlements again, and a person in a long-term, committed, non-marital relationship be deprived of them. In this day and age it beggars belief, but more importantly it calls into question the traditional justifications relied on by the courts in affording marriage greater protection to the detriment of other forms of relationships.

Proponents for reform of the law applicable to cohabitants have long sought to align such relationships with marriage. Common arguments tend to demonstrate the similarities between marriage and such committed relationships. To date these efforts have been in vain. However, the shift in approach now appears to have come from the other side, in that marriage has moved closer towards cohabitation, in that both types of relationships can be terminated by either party unilaterally.

Whilst the introduction of divorce itself brought with it radical legal and social change, it was accompanied with an unforeseen wave of social change in the form of the 'Celtic Tiger'. The last ten years have seen a dramatic increase in economic wealth. There are now approximately 33,000 millionaires living in Ireland. The number of divorced persons in Ireland in 2006 stood at 59,500. Between 2002 and 2006 the number of divorced persons in Ireland increased by 70 per cent, and it now represents the fastest growing marital status. This all points towards a general public acceptance of divorce, and the recognition of a broadening of opinion as to nature and form of socially acceptable relationships. However, a notable feature of these figures is the vast number of people who remain married. Marriage, like life, is seasonal with its good times and its bad times. Despite the stresses and strains of everyday life, people remain committed to one another in a marriage, thus demonstrating the strength and depth of this relationship. As such, marriage can justifiably enjoy a privileged status in society, however, such status should not be to the detriment of other forms of relationships.

The Family and the Constitution

Article 41 of the Constitution recognises the family as the natural and primary unit group of society. The family, for the purposes of the Constitution, is that based on marriage alone. The constitutional family enjoys a privileged status in Irish society, a status which has been fostered and protected by the courts over the years. The origins for this can be traced back to the papal encyclical of Pope Leo XIII, *Rerum Novarum*.

The constitutional family is viewed as an autonomous institution free from outside interference. In terms of issues affecting a particular family it can be accurately described as a micro-sovereignty, in that it is subject to its own rules. The protection afforded to this right by the Irish courts is weighty, to say the least, so much so that it trumped the potential risk to the health of a child in the case of *North Western Health Board v. H.W.*[6] Interestingly, the right to marital privacy was afforded protection before the right to individual privacy. In *McGee v. Attorney General*,[7] the Supreme Court held that s. 17 of the Criminal Law (Amendment) Act 1935, which prohibited the sale and importation of artificial contraceptive devices, was unconstitutional. A four to one majority of the Supreme Court held that such a provision violated the right to marital privacy.

Family Life Today: The Greatest Revolution?

Article 41 read in conjunction with Article 42 of the Constitution operates so as to defend the family from unwarranted interference by the State. This objective must be viewed in light of the attitudes of society some seventy years ago when the Constitution was enacted. The traditional family unit was viewed with reverence and respect. However, in more recent times there have been more calls for interference in this unit in an effort to safeguard individual members, for example, children and elderly members in need of care. Traditionally, it was thought that the Constitution only safeguarded the rights of the family unit, and not the individual members of that unit. This has been the subject of criticism in recent times, particularly in relation to the failure of the Constitution to expressly safeguard the position of the child within the family. Whilst there has been some judicial dicta to the effect that Article 41 also safeguards the rights and interests of individual members of the family, nothing definitive has yet emerged. In addition, there is a growing body of public support in favour of safeguarding the interests of children by way of constitutional amendment. However, this has yet to occur.

Marriage is the basis upon which the constitutional family is formed, there are no additional requirements. Therefore, the stereotypical family unit of a father, mother and 2.4 children is not required. It would appear, for instance, that a married couple without children still constitutes a family for the purposes of Article 41.[8] Similarly, a widow/widower and his/her children constitute a family, as would presumably orphaned siblings. In addition, a family in the throes of marital breakdown, with parents living separately and apart, still benefits from the protections of Article 41 of the Constitution.[9]

In 1937, the Constitution based the family upon marriage. However, in 1937 marriage had a different meaning to that attributed to it today. Prior to 1995, marriage was deemed to be a life-long union between a man and a woman to the exclusion of all others. Following the divorce referendum in 1995, marriage is no longer a life-long union. As a result, the constitutional family has also undergone a change. This redefinition of the family now provides for the situation, whereby two persons who are no longer husband and wife and do not reside with each other and who have children can be categorised as a family for the purposes of the constitution. Yet two people who do reside with each other, but are not married and have children cannot.

The Position of Children

When discussing divorce and separation, the position of the husband and wife is often concentrated on with little or no thought given to a child of the marriage. Children are often the most affected category of persons as a result of marital breakdown. Their feelings of loss, hurt and anger are often compounded by the fact that they feel excluded from the decision-making process. In a sense, children are invisible when it comes to separation and divorce.

The Guardianship of Infants Act, 1964, dictates that in proceedings concerning the upbringing of a child his/her welfare is paramount. However, this does not necessarily appear to be the case in the context of separation or divorce proceedings. Whilst it is acknowledged that there are a number of equally important issues to be determined in such proceedings, the child should still be accorded some level of priority and at the very least have his/her opinion expressed to the court. A child needs to feel involved in the process so as to better understand it. It is no longer acceptable to keep children in the dark in respect of matrimonial litigation that will result in a dramatic change of circumstances for the child. Research evidence suggests that children can adjust to parental separation, but those who cope better tend to feel that their views and perspectives have been taken into account. It is clear that the objective of divorce is to end the relationship between husband and wife, but a child cannot be divorced from his/her parents. This is a point of fundamental importance which needs to be appreciated. In that regard, the viewpoint of the child is critical and needs to be afforded the opportunity to be expressed.

In affording the child the opportunity to partake in the process with a view to better understanding matters, it is important that appropriate safeguards be put in place to protect the child from any animosity between the parents. To that end, it is important to ensure that the child is not used as a shield or a sword by either parent. A court-ordered report of a child psychologist might be a means of achieving this, whereby the report would act as a conduit through which the child voices his/her opinion on matters directly to the judge, thereby avoiding the need to involve the parents.

The Family and the European Convention on Human Rights

Article 8 of the European Convention on Human Rights (ECHR) proclaims the right to respect for private and family life. Whilst the interpretation as to what constitutes a family in Irish law focuses on the form of the relationship, i.e. marriage, the ECHR centres on the substance of the relationship. Indeed, as shall be seen the European Court of Human Rights (ECtHR) has taken a broad and generally inclusive view as to what constitutes a family for the purposes of the convention. No distinction is drawn between a marital and non–marital family. To this end, the ECHR takes a more inclusive approach to family life than the constitution.

Family life for the purposes of the ECHR extends beyond relations between parents and children. In *Boyle v. UK*[10] family life was held to exist between an uncle and nephew; in *Kroon v. The Netherlands*[11] a long-term cohabiting couple with four children constituted a family; and in *Boughanemi v. France*[12] the court held that family life did exist where a father could show a close relationship with a child. The determining factor as to what constitutes a family under the convention is not marriage, but the existence of a real and close family tie. Evidently, it is a question of fact and degree.

The preferential treatment afforded to the family based on marriage under Irish law does not necessarily amount to a breach of the ECHR. It has been held that differential treatment between various forms of relationships may be justified in the interests of protecting the traditional family structure.[13] That said, however, the ECtHR has held that Irish laws in respect of the guardianship rights of unmarried fathers vis-à-vis their children were contrary to the ECHR. In *Keegan v. Ireland*[14] the applicant father was in a relationship with a woman with whom he had a baby. The relationship ended and the mother sought to place the child for adoption. The applicant sought to be consulted in the adoption process. Irish law, as it then stood, did not provide for this and the applicant's case failed before the Irish courts, including the Supreme Court. He then took his case to the ECtHR where it was held that the father's rights under Articles 6 and 8 of the ECHR had been violated. The court held that despite the fact that the natural parents of the child were not married to one another, they still constituted a family for the purposes of the convention.

Possible Reform in this Area

There is an obvious conflict between the Irish interpretation as to what constitutes a family and that of the ECtHR. It is acknowledged that, objectively speaking, marriage is the best predictor as to the stability and commitment of a relationship and as such it may be accorded some prominence in our society. Nonetheless, a legal framework is needed for those who are excluded from that institution. The recognition of relationships outside of marriage does not in and of itself undermine or attack the institution of marriage. Other forms of relationships do not necessarily demean marriage. Indeed, the respect which marriage ought to be accorded is very much an issue for the parties to any given marriage, as opposed to those who are in alternative relationships. The pre-eminence of marriage is dependent on the manner in which it is treated by those a party to it. So as to maintain its respected position, it must be treated with the trust, loyalty and commitment it entails. Provided that is the case, then marriage as an institution will always occupy a prominent role in society. However, if those who are a party to marriage do not treat it with the respect it deserves it will become devalued. Marriage should not be entered into with the end game in sight, i.e. divorce. Divorce is not a mechanism to be used flippantly. It ought to be used as a last resort where a marriage has broken down and there is no prospect of reconciliation. That said, it would appear that the greatest threat to the institution of marriage comes from the inside, as opposed to other forms of relationships. The recognition and accordance of rights, entitlements and privileges to other forms of relationships does not demean our everyday understanding of family life. As Ms Justice L'Heureux-Dubé of the Canadian Supreme Court stated in *Canada v. Mossop*: 'It is possible to be pro-family without rejecting less traditional family forms. It is not anti-family to support protection for non–traditional families'.[15]

The debate as to what constitutes marriage is not solely Irish, rather it is a debate taking place throughout the world. Irrespective of its meaning one thing is clear, the institution of marriage needs to be supported. Marriage still represents the relationship paradigm from which unity, stability, commitment and interdependence flows. It must be treated in a real and positive manner. With the rights and entitlements which accompany marriage there are also duties and obligations which need to be adhered to.

The public support for reform in this area is apparent and has recently manifested itself in the form of the Civil Partnership Bill 2008. The Bill proposes to establish a new form of registered civil partnership for same-sex couples and a redress scheme for long-term cohabiting couples and same-sex couples. A scheme of civil partnership is not proposed for opposite sex couples on the basis that it would compete with the institution of marriage and as such may be interpreted as an attack on that institution. These difficulties do not arise in the context of same-sex couples due to the fact that they are not entitled to marry under Irish law, therefore, the provision for an alternative form of relationship cannot be seen as a disincentive to marry, having regard to the fact that they are precluded from so doing.

To benefit from the civil partnership scheme the parties must 'opt in', meaning that they must register their partnership. This is a public ceremony not all too different to a civil marriage. It is open to persons aged eighteen years and above with sufficient mental competence. The parties must be of the same sex and not be close relatives. At the time of the ceremony neither party may be married or in another civil partnership. Similar to marriage, three months' notice must be provided of the parties' intention to engage in the ceremony.

The proposed cohabitation scheme operates on a presumptive basis, i.e. it may apply to all cohabitants without the need for them to demonstrate additional factors. The Bill draws a distinction between 'cohabitants' and 'qualified cohabitants'. All cohabitants will be entitled to seek relief under the Domestic Violence Acts, the Civil Liability Acts, the Power of Attorney Act, 1996, and the Residential Tenancies Act, 2004.

Family Life Today: The Greatest Revolution?

'Qualified cohabitants' are defined as persons who have lived together for three years, or two years where there are children of the relationship. A qualified cohabitant may claim from the estate of a deceased partner. In the event of the relationship breaking down, economically dependent qualified cohabitants may claim:

- maintenance;
- accommodation; and
- pension rights.

It is also proposed that where cohabitants share a home, regardless as to who owns it, a partner is not permitted to sell, lease or mortgage the property without the prior written consent of the other partner. The proposed scheme provides that cohabitants can opt out of the provisions therein by way of a cohabitation agreement. Notwithstanding this, such an agreement may be set aside by a court in exceptional circumstances where its enforcement would cause serious injustice.

Assisted Reproductive Technologies – A New Dawn with New Challenges

People who wish to have families but have been unable to do so have embraced the development of assisted reproductive technologies (ARTs). Such technologies provide people with a renewed sense of hope in having children. However, a number of social, legal and ethical issues arise. It is not intended to deal with these issues in the present paper. Indeed, to do so would not do justice to the complexity and weight of the issues involved. Rather, it is proposed to raise a number of the issues which have a bearing on legal matters concerning the family.

A preliminary issue arises as to the manner in which the

availability and use of ARTs should be regulated, if at all. Should there be a limit as to who might avail of these facilities, for example, should they be confined to married heterosexual couples, cohabiting couples, single parents, or same-sex couples? Due to the absence of legislative regulation in this area these questions remain unanswered. The immediate and present effect of this is that clinics providing ARTs do so in a varied manner. The manner of assessment of potential applicants is obviously an issue of grave importance, yet it is unregulated at present. Can every applicant who presents themselves to such a clinic demonstrate that it would be in the best interests of the potential child to be born to them? Moreover, is the best interests of the child test an appropriate approach to take? Persons who seek to adopt a child must undergo a suitability and eligibility assessment, but there is no such obligation at present on applicants for ARTs to undertake a similar assessment. The ability to pose these questions coupled with the inability to provide answers illustrates the need to address our minds as a society to this issue. One thing that is certain is that time, effort and thought needs to be put into this issue, because the current position is untenable.

ARTs now make it possible for a child to have five parents: the sperm donor, egg donor, surrogate mother and two parents who care for the child or possibly adopt it. A variety of issues can arise in this regard including parentage, custody, access and the manner in which the family unit is to be defined. In the recent High Court case of *J.McD. v. P.L. and B.M.*,[16] Hedigan J. considered a guardianship and access application brought by a homosexual man who donated his sperm to a lesbian couple. The couple had been in a relationship since 1996 and entered into a civil union in the United Kingdom in 2006. In refusing the application, Hedigan J. held that the welfare of the child was best served by remaining under the care and control of the lesbian couple, with the applicant father having no rights of guardianship, custody or access. It is noted, however, that this matter was appealed to the Supreme Court and judgment has been reserved.

Conclusion

Over a half a century ago in Trinity College, Dublin, Dr A.L. Goodhart, then Master of University College, Oxford, commented on the need to regularly ensure that our laws keep apace with the practical realities of everyday life:

> The law must, as far as possible, mirror contemporary civilization and as that changes so must the law. If the law becomes too rigid and inflexible, then there is always the danger that it will be in conflict with the needs of the people, with all the unfortunate consequences to which such a conflict may give rise.[17]

Many people would argue that Irish family law has failed to keep abreast with the modern practical family unit. The Constitution focuses on the nuclear marital family and does not countenance other family forms outside of this. Whilst law reform will not itself alter socio-structural realities, it can provide the impetus for wider social reforms. It is submitted that a large portion, if not the majority, of society through its actions has demonstrated the need to provide some protection for non-traditional family units. There are now some fifty-two thousand children residing with cohabiting couples. Should it not be said that these children are members of a family? Have we now come to the point where one can justifiably state that the law and justice are conflicting concepts in the context of the rights of family units?

In conclusion, we need to place greater emphasis on family support. We need to develop increased, effective and flexible services to support children and families experiencing difficulties. Family support services play a vital role in contributing to the future well-being of children and families. We need to invest in services where people can learn about relationships and parenting skills. We need greater investment in systems and supports for marriage and relationships. We need to support those marriages that are capable of being saved. We need to enable those which cannot be saved to be dissolved with the minimum of avoidable distress, bitterness and hostility. In short, we need to minimise the bitterness and distress engendered by the divorce process. We need to encourage, so far as possible, the amicable resolution of practical issues relating to the couple's home, finances and children and the proper discharge of their responsibilities to one another and to their children. We should seek to minimise the harm that the children of the family may suffer, both at the time of the divorce and in the future, and to promote, so far as possible, the continued sharing of parental responsibility for them.

Divorce disputes need alternative forms of dispute resolution other than the courts, although it must be said that the courts are needed for cases that cannot be resolved in any other manner. Alternative Dispute Resolution (ADR) mechanisms at least aspire to promote consensus rather than conflict, which is particularly important for the welfare and dignity of the children, the subjects of divorce proceedings.

In addition, with regards to more comfortable, convenient and client-friendly court facilities, both the courts and parties to a divorce would benefit greatly from the promotion and more widespread use of mediation, collaborative law and other forms of alternative dispute resolution. This should be realised through more robust legislation facilitating alternative dispute resolution, which would minimise the number of contested cases ending up in the courts, and also reduce the level of

Family Life Today: The Greatest Revolution?

'brinkmanship' that sees many settlements being reached on the steps of the courts.

Notes

1   Gary, Susan, 'Adapting Intestacy Laws to Changing Families', *Law and Inequality,* XVIII, No.1 (2000), p. 80.
2   Herman Hill, Kay, 'Private Choices and Public Policy: Confronting the Limitations of Marriage', *Australian Journal of Family Law,* Vol. 5, No. 69 (1991), p. 85.
3   [1966] I.R. 567.
4   [1984] I.R. 316.
5   [1996] 1 I.R. 426.
6   [2001] 3 I.R. 635.
7   [1974] I.R. 284.
8   *Murray v. Ireland* [1985] I.L.R.M. 542, at 546, per Costello J.
9   *T.F. v. Ireland* [1995] 1 I.R. 321.
10 [1994] 19 E.H.R.R. 233.
11 [1994] 19 E.H.R.R. 263.
12 Application No. 22070/93, 24 April, 1996.
13 *Saucedo Gomez v. Spain,* Application No. 37784/97, 26 January, 1999.
14 [1994] 18 E.H.R.R. 342.
15 [1993] 100 D.L.R. (4th) 858, p. 712.
16 [2008] I.E.H.C. 96 (Unreported, High Court, Hedigan J., 16 April, 2008).
17 Goodhart, A.L., *Law Reform – Judicial and Legislative*, (11 May, 1954), Dublin University Press Ltd.

Home and School

Changing Family Patterns: Altruism as the Greatest Revolution

Marie Murray
Clinical Psychologist and Health Columnist for the *Irish Times*

The changes in family patterns in Ireland are well documented. Census figures from 2006 show the extent of change in the past two decades. There has been an increase of 80% in the number of lone-parent families; one-fifth of children are now in a lone-parent family form, a form that is four times more likely to live in poverty than others. More than one-third of children are born outside of marriage. Marriage may precede parenthood or parenthood may precede marriage, while patterns of cohabitation may precede both parenthood and marriage, so that the family may take a variety of forms. Cohabiting couples are now the fastest growing family unit in the state, with a rise of 60% in half a decade. One-quarter of children are raised in non-marital families and an increasing number of children live with same-sex parents. The number of children being taken into care through the courts has tripled in the past four years and supervision orders have doubled, showing how much families need support.

Two hundred thousand adults have experienced marital breakdown and the number of people availing of divorce has risen by 70% in the past decade. Family configurations are increasingly complex, whereby children living together may be those of first, second or subsequent relationships of one or more of their parents. These children may scatter to different households at weekends to join their 'other parent', while one or more children of the current arrangement are left behind. Sometimes those children are joined in their home by children of former relationships of one of their own parents. This can be confusing in terms of identity, security, stability, family cohesion and extended family relationships.

Depending on circumstances, family arrangements may seem to children to be temporary, home being where and with whom they currently live, subject to adult decisions over which they have no control. While there has been much research on the psychological impact of changing family constitutions on children,[6] the long-term sociological implications for child-rearing practices in this country will remain indeterminate until a number of generations of these fluid family forms enter into their own adult relationship commitments and parenting roles.

Perspectives on Family Patterns

The traditional two-parent, separate-gendered, nuclear family is now just one family configuration amongst many. How one views this and changing family patterns depends on a variety of factors: personal family of origin experiences; experience of being parented; religious beliefs; current marital status; and relationship history. Additionally, most people have a personal ideological position with regards to parenting principles and ideal family forms, with a dominant belief about the conditions most conducive to child development, adolescent security, adult stability, relationship constancy and ideas about personal rights, individual happiness and community welfare. We form ideas about what is best based on our own experiences – good and bad.

It is helpful if we know where we come from psychologically, why we think what we do, what shaped our perspectives, whether or not our ideas are useful and the potential biases in the beliefs that we hold, particularly if we are in any position of authority where prejudices may transmit themselves to children, be it through teaching, social control, therapeutic or other work with different family forms. The range of beliefs about children, parents, parenting practices and families is extensive, and unless we acknowledge and address its complexity and changing patterns and our own position in these many discourses, we may lose sight of how to help families who need help.

Along the continuum of beliefs about families, there are those who welcome the current ease and flux of family life, those who despise its disregard for childhood, those who believe that child development is compromised by its diversity and those who see that their task is to work with people who need support, regardless of how they conduct their lives. There are those who believe that the personality of the child is liberated by multiplicity in relationships and life experiences. They say that what is required most in childhood is a secure environment with stable, well-adjusted parents and a society that ensures equality of respect, opportunity, educational access, societal acceptance and practical support. The 'truths' are in dispute.

What is certain, however, is that whatever one's view of the variety of family structures, it is important that children from these structures are not disrespected. There is an ethical imperative on us to validate people rather than denigrate the choices children's parents make. We have an unfortunate history of doing so. When that happens, the child is burdened with a view of him/herself as being lesser than others, of their parents' martial status being unacceptable and of their living conditions and family interactions as inferior.

Psychology and Family Patterns

One cannot deny that psychology has traditionally emphasised that the best environment for children to grow up in is in a united, two-parent, separate-gendered, stable, loving family form, with transgenerational access to grandparents and extended family. However, psychology has been equally clear about the dangers of blind subscription to the nuclear family in those situations where families of that form are neglectful, abusive, violent or unsafe for children's psychological and physical development. Again, there have been too many instances of children who suffered because their parents' rights were protected, while the children's protection was neglected.

Of course, psychology has also expressed concern for family forms that impose too many adaptations, ruptures of relationships, confusion of identity and instability on children, or that deprive them of sufficient time with their own mothers or fathers and their right to grow up with appropriate guidance and protection from adults. Children have the right to have their formative years as predictable, secure and stable as possible.

Family Therapy and Family Patterns

Family Therapy as a discipline has traditionally emphasised the importance of context and meaning in how families construe themselves and how they are viewed by others. The conditions for family functioning are greatest when the family has insight into its history, its transgenerational experiences and beliefs, its current communication and its evolving relationships with family members, as they negotiate their way through the stability and changes of the life-cycle stages with which they are all engaged together.[7] As children leave home and establish their own families, have their own children, who in time grow up and leave them, the delicacy of the intimacy and weave of life and the family life cycle becomes apparent. Even the most traditional family is one that is constantly shifting, evolving, changing, adapting and adjusting as life progresses; as children are born and grow and depart; as older members die and others step into the front line in life and death.

Children's Perspectives on Family Patterns

Clinically, there is a wealth of information from psychology and family therapy about the impact of family patterns on children.[8] We have the traditional understanding that it is better to live in a loving home with one parent than in a war zone with two. We have heard the emotional responses of children to separation and divorce: their sadness, their separation anxiety, fear of further abandonment, concern for the non-custodial parent and misplaced feelings of guilt and self-blame at having, as children often see it, driven the other parent away. We know about their suppressed rage at parents when they seem to split up in a cavalier fashion on the whim of their own wishes. We know about post-divorce change in school performance, how concentration, application and motivation are often affected, about children's embarrassment telling their schoolmates. We know the host of emotional sequelae that visit children in the aftermath of their parents splitting up.

We have accounts of the difficulties for those children whose parents continue to live together in situations of domestic violence, where they must collude with the family persona that all is well when it is not. We have clear understanding of the anger and angst of adolescents whose parents part and how they agonise when a parent enters a new relationship, because they are put in the bizarre competitive situation of trying to discover their own adolescent sexual identity while their parents, whose sexuality they prefer to be invisible to them, are also rediscovering their sexual selves again with new partners. This puts parents and young people at dissonant life cycle stages. We must remember that, in the preferred thinking of most adolescents, if they ever allow themselves to think about their parents having sex, then it should have been confined to the noble cause of begetting them, after which no further engagement was required.

We understand a great deal about the grief that children feel when a parent leaves home. We know how they suffer when a parent does not maintain contact: the loss, the shattering of attachment and the sense of abandonment. We know how children are usually perturbed when a new child is born to a parent in a new relationship. We are aware of the rupture of relationships if a parent has sequential partners, if a child feels neglected by their mother's or father's partner, or treated differently to that partner's own child living in the family home. We are aware from clinical discussion of the delicacy of children's sensibilities and how deeply they are wounded in childhood when they feel unloved, neglected, disregarded or betrayed.

Because of children's experiences, as they are recounted by them, we need to engage in the depth of sociological analysis that would inform us about how to preserve family life and how to support families. We need to know more about the social and economic conditions and societal changes and discourses that have brought about such systemic societal structural changes, as have been witnessed in families in recent times. In the interim, while what one might call 'The Family' may be on the decline, we need ways to traverse and support all children in all 'Families' and in every family form, so that children are equipped with the resilience of belief in themselves, respect for others, participation in the community and the feelings of self-worth that derive from community involvement.

Altruism

One of the distinguishing characteristics of children in challenging family forms is that they often feel that they do not belong anywhere, that they do not have a role in life that is important, and so they often lose a sense of their own identity, purpose and meaning. They frequently say that they are a burden to others, a drain on family finances (particularly when there are disputes between parents about maintenance). They often see themselves as a problem to be solved with regards to where they live and with whom. They do not see themselves as gifts to society.

If there is one thing that a child needs when its needs are not being met, it is to belong to someone or something and to have a role in life. This is where giving children the joy of altruism, that extraordinary consciousness of the needs of others, can give them a sense of self-esteem, worth and purpose in life. It can provide them with a belief that who they are and what they do has positive meaning for other people and that they have value and a contribution to make to the world.

Introducing children to altruism may be an important therapeutic and significant psychological intervention when life is difficult for them. Although altruism may be viewed as a philosophical disposition, as an ideological principal, or as an abstract and unpractical approach to the needs of children, when it is modelled, nurtured into a personal value system, assisted into practical activity and given appropriate expression in a community, the consequence is a binding with others and growth in the child of a sense of personal value and relevance. A child who is without self-esteem may receive it from giving to others. That is the paradox; that is its power; that is its simple rationale. Prosocial behaviour promotes self-esteem. Therefore, if we ask what will assist children in coping with the diversity of family life today, inviting them to be altruistic may be one way of assisting them. It is one perspective, one parenting precept, one potential means of social cohesion: an emotional and behavioural approach that deserves careful consideration at this time. In this 'Great Revolution' of family life, simple, gentle attention to altruism may be the key.[9]

Altruism and Inspiration

Altruism is usually defined as 'behaviour motivated by concern for others, by internalised values and goals, rather than expectation of social rewards or motivated by the desire to avoid punishment or sanctions.' It is not an arid love but one that we often associate with the heroic images of figures such as Martin Luther King, Mahatma Gandhi, Mother Teresa and those who have maximised this potential within themselves and others. I believe that it is a disposition in every newborn child. If we source it, encourage it, develop it and nurture it, we nurture the child, all the people with whom that child will interact, the local community and society as a whole, throughout that child's life and the later lives of his or her children into future generations.

Altruism is not just acts of consideration, kindness or charity; it is a way of living. It is an emotional disposition. It is a practical approach. It is a special human form of responsibility to the other. It is not contrived, designed, marketed, nor is it a technique or a behaviourist approach to child rearing. It does not depend on systems of reward or punishment but contains within itself its own reward. It is gentle. It is spiritual. It is transcendent. It lifts children out of egocentricity. It takes adolescents away from egoism and puts adults back in touch with the finer aspects of themselves.

Altruism is a gift received as it is given. It is deeply respectful of the fragility and delicacy of the child's sensibilities. It is aware of how wonderful adolescents may be if we believe in them. It is wishing to contribute beyond oneself. It is not a 'selfish gene'[10] it is a genuine human emotion. It inspires the young, makes young adults conscious of their good luck if they have been privileged, makes them aware of their educational advantage if they have been so gifted and allows them to understand the obligations of privilege, advantage, youth and the capacity to love. Altruism has proven benefits in all settings: educational, social, emotional and family life. It dismantles conflict. It imbues interactions in diverse family configurations, educational settings and community endeavours with meaning. Because it gives meaning to interactions it gives meaning to life. And life as we enter a recession requires meaning, requires review, requires hope, requires sharing and communitarian ethics, contributions from everyone and especially the idealism, energy and enthusiasm of those who are young.

Social Learning Theory

Social learning theory shows how children learn altruism.[11] They do so through their observations and social interactions, through adults modelling ideal behaviour which they can emulate, through opportunities to experience themselves as competent carers and when they discover their own capacities to help others.[12] Conversations that promote altruism as a way of living encourage altruistic behaviour. Positive parenting styles encourage the development of prosocial behaviours that have an altruistic base. Altruism is learned from parents and significant adults. Children learn altruism because they witness it. They learn altruism because it speaks to something integral in them: their own natural loving potential with which they arrive into the world and which, sadly, is often contaminated, diluted, or destroyed before it finds expression in their lives.

One of the concerns that many psychologists and family therapists have is the possible impact on the child who experiences ruptures of attachment[13] on their later play and social skills, their capacity for empathy, development of conscience, self-control, social behaviour, self-esteem, relationships and later parenting capacity. Children and adolescents without encouragement, in their loss of hope, idealism and belief, can turn to the least helpful contexts for support: the gang or the group that are equally angry and disenchanted with life. Parenting programmes that support parents and social programmes that give young people opportunities to be altruistic towards other people, to share their time, their talents, their company, their abilities and their concern, are inspirational. The election of the first black President of the United States, which coincided with the 2008 Céifin Conference, confirms for us that looking outwards rather than inwards, being positive rather than pessimistic, giving generously and altruistically works, and that despite early disadvantage, the power of setting one's sights on what seems to be impossible is possible and brings results. What we take today from the election of Barack Obama is demonstration that change, however daunting it may seem, is possible. In times of recession, however bleak they may be, change can come about if we believe in ourselves and help young people to say, 'Yes we can'.[14]

Altruism and Hope

For many of us who work clinically, there is one constant in the flux of life, one iridescent message of hope, one exceptional shining psychological light: the extraordinary inherent, powerful capacity of the child to love its caregivers; to attach, to bond, to form close relationships with those in its orbit; and, except in cases of extreme adult pathology, to create and evoke what is best in human nature and what is most important for the survival of our species in noble form. Children love their parents; their parents love them – altruism may ultimately connect each of us to the other.

Psychology and anthropological researcher Warneken[15] shows how the tiny child, as early as eighteen months of age, displays that most magnificent of human capacities: the capacity for altruistic behaviour, giving, sharing and caring without gain. What this demonstrates is that parent–child relationships are not about technique, but about love. While behaviourist approaches to parenting may produce child compliance, and cognitive behaviour programmes for adolescents may provide insight into negative patterns of thinking and doing, there is a transformative power to fostering altruism that supersedes psychoeducational technique. The seminal work by researcher Eisenberg on *The Caring Child*[16] and the benefits of altruism alert us to the importance of eliciting those prosocial behaviours already within the child.

Those of us privileged to work with young people, as I do with university students, see their yearning for meaning, for relevance, for sense and shape to their world. Many of them find it in altruism. Young people run the 'Goal Mile' on Christmas Day; go to the RDS to serve meals to those without homes; they walk the Camino de Santiago to support disadvantaged youth; they volunteer in large numbers overseas using their physical strength and intellectual prowess for others; they sleep out in the cold and rain, not just collecting for homelessness, but living, for a week or more, the reality of having nowhere but the ground to sleep on during winter time. They have within them so much that we do not acknowledge enough or extract from them sufficiently. They wish to give. They are generous beyond belief. When their idealism, energy, instinctive goodness, altruism and spirituality are touched they respond. We do young people a disservice if we do not expect the best of them, because they are, truly, the best of us.

When we speak about violence in society, about the demise of social structures, about the breakdown of family life, about the economic recession, and predict a grim global future for us all, it may be worth remembering that one of the solutions may lie within us in our untapped capacity 'to give and not to count the cost'. Imagine that to nurture the child, to validate what is most splendid in adolescence and to encourage what is most gracious in adulthood, we may simply need to return to the gentleness of altruism. Can we do it? We can do it, 'Yes we can'.

Notes

1   Based on 2006 Census analysis, *Marriage Breakdown and Family Structure in Ireland*, September 2007, the Iona Institute.

2   *Irish Times,* 'HEALTHplus', Genevieve Carbury, 2 September 2008, p. 3.

3   McKeown, K., *Family Well-Being*, commissioned by the Céifin Centre, 2003.

4   *Irish Times,* 'Home News', Carl O'Brien, 31 October 2008, p.3.

5   *Irish Times,* 'HEALTHplus', Fiona Garland, 2 September 2008, p. 3.

6   Wallerstein, J. S. and Kelly, J.B., *Surviving the Break-up: How Children and Parents Cope with Divorce*, New York: Basic Books, 1980.

7   Hoffman, L., 'Constructing The Theoretical Context: A Reflexive Stance for Family Therapy' in S. McNamee and K.J. Gergen (eds), *Therapy as Social Construction,* London: Sage Publications, 1992, p. 7–24. Also, McGoldrick, M. and Gerson, R., *Genograms in Family Assessment,* New York: Norton, 1985.

8   Murray, M. and Keane, C., *The Teenage Years,* Cork: Mercier Press, 1997.

9   *Irish Times,* 'Opinion and Analysis', Marie Murray, 5 November 2008, p. 13.

10 Dawkins, R., *The Selfish Gene*, Oxford: Oxford University Press, 2006.

11 This has been shown since the 1960s, as well as in work by writers such as Bandura A. and Waters, R., *Social Learning and Personality Development*, New York: Holt, Rinehart & Winston, 1963. Social Learning Theory has informed debates about what societal models and media representations teach the child.

12 There are too many writers in the area to cite, but see especially Berkowitz, M.W. and Grytch, J.H., 'Fostering Goodness: Teaching Parents to Facilitate Children's Moral Development', *Journal of Moral*

Education, 1998, Vol. 27 No. 3, pp. 371–391.

13   See the seminal work of John Bowlby and Mary Ainsworth in Bowlby, J., *Maternal Care and Mental Health,* World Health Organisation, Vol. 14, 1951. See also Bowlby, J., *The Making and Breaking of Affectional Bonds,* London: Routledge Classics, 2005.

14   Campaign slogan of Democratic Candidate Barack Obama, elected to the Presidency of America on 4 November 2008, was 'Yes we can'. Position one of promoting a communitarian ethic and serving others as the way to support the self.

15   Warneken, F. and Tomasello, M., *The Origins of Human Altruism – Integrating Developmental and Comparative Perspectives*, proceedings from the Jean Piaget Society Meeting, Amsterdam.

16   Eisenberg, N., *The Caring Child*, Cambridge, MA: Harvard University Press, 1992. Also Eisenberg, N. and Mussen, P.H., *The Roots of Prosocial Behaviour in Children*, Cambridge: Cambridge University Press, 1989.

Patrick Hillery in Context

John Quinn
Author and Former Senior Producer with RTÉ Radio 1

It is fitting that the 2008 Céifin Conference honours Patrick Hillery for his contribution to Irish educational policy and development, and I am privileged to be part of that tribute. When Céifin began ten years ago, two regular attendees each year were Patrick Hillery and Brendan O'Regan: two great Clare men whom we have sadly lost in the past year.

Let me take you back to 1959. Waterford won the All-Ireland Hurling final, Kerry won the football title – and John Quinn did the Leaving Cert! What career options were open to him? Not university. Teaching maybe? The Civil Service? The Bank? He opted for teaching, and with the help of St Joseph of Cupertino he got his wish. On the bigger stage, a few months earlier, Ken Whitaker's Economic Development had been published. This would lead to the First Programme for Economic Expansion, an approach in which the Fianna Fáil government's economic policy looked outward to the world, a reversal of Eamon de Valera's inward-looking policy. De Valera became president and Seán Lemass became Taoiseach. Among his cabinet was a thirty-one year old GP from Milltown Malbay, Co. Clare. He had been a reluctant TD and now he was Minister for Education.

We were on the eve of a new decade: the 1960s would be swinging and sexy; a technological revolution was on the way; Sputnik was already in space; in two years' time we would have our own television service; and, if we were to believe Oliver J. Flanagan, TD, we would have sex for the first time! It was an interesting time to be appointed Minister for Education. An opening, expanding economy would demand a more open and expanded educational system. Soon we would hear phrases like 'investment in education' and 'equality of educational opportunity'. They are commonplace now, but were not then.

So 1959 was very much a transition point in terms of educational policy. Up to then it had been dominated by Eamon de Valera and Tomás Deirg. The revival of the Irish language had been a major plank in that policy, but otherwise there had been little involvement. Now there were young tigers about: Hillery, Colley and O'Malley. Things would change in the new optimism and pragmatism of the Lemass years.

In particular, it fell to Patrick Hillery to outline the way forward, which he did for the next six years (he was the longest serving Minister of Education in the past fifty years).

Economic expansion meant greater financial commitment to education. Lemass said to Hillery, 'You write it and I'll say it, put a sentence in my Ard-Fheis speech'. It was done. The money was there and there was no scarcity of ways to spend it. Patrick Hillery wanted to broaden secondary education and develop technological education. The whole question of higher education provision needed to be investigated, and to that end a Commission on Higher Education was set up in 1960. It took seven years to issue its report, which was quite damning, but the seeds were sown. (In one interview in 2000, Dr Hillery said we were educating for failure in the 1960s. The seminaries got the pick of the crop – then teaching, then the Civil Service. The rest were 'failures'. They didn't fail the Leaving Cert. They failed to get the top places.)

Patrick Hillery's ministry was a proactive one, even though he would never claim to be an educationalist. In 1963 he gave a major speech, which outlined many of the seminal ideas on educational reform, which would come to fruition throughout the 1960s. Among them, he proposed:

- A new type of school, the comprehensive school, which would be coeducational and open to all levels of ability, with a wide-ranging curriculum, to be located where there had been a lack of post-primary schools;
- The two-year course in vocational schools would be extended to three years and a wider Inter Cert course would be offered to secondary and vocational schools;
- A technical Leaving Cert would be introduced;
- Regional Technical Colleges (now Institutes of Technology) would be set up to help align educational provision with manpower needs.

In that same year – 1963 – there was another innovation that might seem small now, but was of great importance to me as a young teacher: the introduction of a basic reference library for primary schools.

All of these changes were not universally welcomed. The notion of greater government involvement in education didn't go down well with some bishops. For example, witness these exchanges between Dr Hillery and Dr Browne of Galway:

Dr B: You are changing education.
Dr H: How is the golf, my Lord?
Dr B: You are making big changes in education?
Dr H: Are you golfing at all my Lord?
(He got the message. I wasn't going to talk.)

There is an image of Patrick Hillery as a reticent, tentative minister. In itself this might not be a bad thing, but a better description is that of 'a thoughtful, questioning man'. That came from Patrick Lynch, who was appointed Director of the OECD analysis of Irish education, which Dr Hillery set up in 1962. This would examine provision, participation and projections for the future.

Its 1966 Report, *Investment in Education,* is one of the foundation documents of modern Irish education. Patrick Lynch told me Dr Hillery would often sit in on an OECD session, but would never make a direct contribution. Rather, he would throw in a particularly awkward question, which would make you go away and think for a week in search of an answer.

The OECD report was disturbing. It forecast serious deficiencies in the numbers holding certificates, especially in technically-qualified personnel. From a cohort of 55,000 pupils, 17,500 left school at primary certificate level and 11,000 of those left without a primary certificate. Of the 37, 500 who did go to second level, over a third dropped out without sitting for a further certificate. Of the 10,000 who sat the Leaving Certificate, only 2,000 went on to university. There were huge discrepancies in participation in education with regards to social class and geographical distribution. Maths and science teaching were very under-resourced. Continental languages were very poorly served (98 per cent of boys did Latin at Inter Cert and 88 per cent did Latin at Leaving Cert).

We were a long, long way back, but at least we were beginning to know it. Patrick Hillery was ploughing and harrowing and sowing seeds. Fruition came later, notably with the free education system introduced by his flamboyant successor, Donogh O'Malley. But the Quiet Man had done the spadework in terms of examining the system. He had also introduced many practical measures:

- Better maintenance provision for national schools;
- Reduction of class size;

- Increased capacity in St Patrick's Training College;
- Promotion of maths and science through curricular reform, in-service education and differential teacher salaries;
- Encouragement of modern languages;
- Capital building grants to private secondary schools;
- A modified scholarship scheme for higher education;
- Resources to relocate University College Dublin to Belfield;
- Libraries in national schools.

Six long years. Six challenging years. Six difficult years. A lot done. A lot more to do. And it would be done; done under the stewardship of a reluctant minister, a non-educationalist but a quiet man, fiercely committed to equality of opportunity, for whom the phrase 'cherishing all the children of the nation equally' was a personal passion and not an empty political cliché.

Céifin salutes and thanks Dr Patrick Hillery with the 2008 Céifin Award, presented to his widow Maeve Hillery by Bishop Willie Walsh.

Home and School: The Patrick Hillery Memorial Lecture

Mary Forde
Principal of Presentation College, Athenry, Co. Galway

I am deeply honoured to present the Patrick Hillery Memorial Lecture. Sincere thanks to Fr Harry Bohan for the invitation to deliver the lecture at the 2008 Céifin Conference.

A constant theme running through the Céifin Conferences since 1998 has been the changes in family life. 'What,' asks Fr Harry Bohan in the Céifin brochure, 'does the family contribute to human, social and spiritual development?' It is my task to look particularly at the family and the connections between the home and school.

First, I will look at the main structural features of the Irish school system. Attendance at full-time education in Ireland is compulsory for children between six and sixteen years of age. The vast majority of Irish children (about 98%) attend non-fee-paying, publicly-funded primary schools (referred to until recently as national schools). This publicly-funded school system consists of eight years of primary schooling (including two years of infant education between the age of four and six). This is followed by five or six years of second level or post-primary schooling – three years of junior cycle and either two or three years of senior cycle. Almost 95% of pupils enrolled in post-primary schools attend publicly-funded secondary, vocational, comprehensive or community schools that are non-fee-paying.

There are just under 450,000 children enrolled in 3,157 primary schools in Ireland, taught by 26,282 teachers. There are

Family Life Today: The Greatest Revolution?

742 second-level schools in Ireland comprising 403 secondary schools (54% of total), 247 vocational schools and community colleges (33% of total) and 92 community and comprehensive schools (13% of total). There are 335,162 pupils enrolled in these schools, taught by 24,990 teachers.

In considering the relationships between home and school, I will look at the relationship as follows:

1 What has changed?
2 What should change?
3 What can change?

As my experiences have been mainly at second-level, I will consider the home and school relationship in that sector.

What Has Changed?

The world changes and Irish homes and schools change with it. Over the past decade, the Irish economic scene has changed significantly. The rate of change has been accelerating over recent decades and will probably continue to do so. While the buoyant economy has resulted in significant income increases for a large proportion of the Irish population, the number living below the poverty line remains unacceptably high. There continues to be a significant disparity between the educational attainment of those from higher socio-economic backgrounds and those from less advantaged homes and backgrounds. The rate of early school leaving, especially among those from less advantaged backgrounds, continues to be high. In spite of a series of initiatives by government to encourage and support students to remain on in school, about 18% of the age cohort leave school every year without completing senior cycle secondary school. And while, overall, 65% of those who complete second level school proceed to further or higher education, there are glaring disparities in access to higher education, with students from the most advantaged homes and backgrounds having third-level participation rates up to four times higher than those from disadvantaged homes.

In general, there is a positive attitude towards education in Ireland. Both providers and participants believe in the value and importance of education. While it is recognised that there is scope for improvement, the quality of the Irish education system is highly regarded: 'Ireland's schools are largely seen to produce the goods, in terms of measurable grades' (OECD, 2003). An on-going concern, however, is that the system is not catering for the needs of all pupils (approximately 18% leave school before completing the senior cycle). During the past decade, the State has introduced a number of initiatives, including curriculum reform and other interventions, to support students to remain in school until the completion of the Leaving Certificate examination and to achieve their academic potential. However, to date these initiatives have not achieved the hoped-for outcomes and the proportion of pupils who drop out of full-time schooling before sitting the Leaving Certificate remains the same today as it was fifteen years ago.

In addition, the economic, social and cultural background of students attending Irish schools is changing rapidly. Students present to schools with alternative lifestyles and varying expectations. School leaders need to reflect on how they can support and empower staff, students and parents in this changing environment. While the Irish economy is buoyant, there are families living in poverty. Schools are also expected to deal with family breakdown, abuse of drugs, obesity and other social issues. Schools are often seen as the centre of the community – a place where people turn in times of crisis. In this context, schools now deal with many external agencies, for example, social services, health officials, psychologists and Gardaí.

Schools are increasingly enrolling pupils with a wide variety of educational needs. The school population in Ireland has become more diverse and this trend is likely to continue. Arising from the major increase in immigration to Ireland in recent years, schools now cater for a level of cultural, ethnic, religious, linguistic and intellectual diversity, which is unprecedented. In addition, school enrolments include a growing number of pupils from the Traveller community, whose school attendance in the past was sporadic and irregular. The inclusion of children with special educational needs in mainstream classrooms adds to the diversity within the classroom. A culture of inclusion in schools requires that all pupils are respected and supported and their needs met.

Newcomer children (not born in Ireland), whether asylum seekers, convention or programme refugees, or children of migrant workers, between four and eighteen have the same right to primary and post-primary education as the rest of the Irish population, and are required to attend school between the ages of six and sixteen. Schools have a pivotal role to play in integrating the newcomer students into schools and into society by developing a more inclusive, intercultural classroom environment and providing children with the knowledge and skills they need to participate in the multicultural Ireland of today.

Traditionally, the family and home is the schoolroom of life; parents are the primary educators passing on virtues of self-discipline. As outlined, this is a period of significant change in Ireland – in schools and schooling, and in relationships between home and school. Historically, the family was viewed as a foundation of society. The assumption was that a good family is the real schoolroom for life, the place where you learn the lessons of self-discipline, the handling of relationships and care for others, the rewards of work and the need of learning. (This was outlined in Fr Harry Bohan's book, *Hope Begins at Home*.)

This ideal situation is happening for some children. Yet social change results in many being deprived of this background. Increasingly, schools are forced to take on the role of parents: to feed, to clothe, to provide emotional support and to offer guidance to children and their families. I can recount stories from my colleagues and myself where, in our daily work, it is not unusual:

- To provide breakfast, dinner and supper to children;
- To go to court and keep a student out of prison;
- To pay for school trips and visits;
- To offer help in parents' separations;
- To intervene to assist children in broken homes;
- To offer counselling;
- To visit children in institutional care;
- To support children in care where the parent does not wish to offer support.

There is no doubt that much of the economic and social change has been good. In general, people have seen better opportunities in education. However, some aspects of change have done little for the lives of some individuals, families, communities and, in some cases, schools. The scourges of unemployment, emigration, segregation and widespread poverty have disappeared, but not from all homes. The tragic stories of physical and sexual abuse have been aired. In many aspects of life improvements have been made; we have had new homes, new truths, newcomers and new hope. There have been huge levels of success and yet all is not in order as we look at our children in our schools.

This conference allows time to stop and look closely at the choices we are making, which will shape family life into the future. It allows us to look back and evaluate ourselves around the creative reforms and initiatives put in place by Paddy Hillery when he set about offering free education to all. Sadly, in times of phenomenal change we have lost sight as a society of a values-driven education. We are indifferent to completion of our journey and deaf to the voices of the excluded. We must acknowledge our duty to care for the weak, allowing everyone a fair chance – especially a chance in education.

Indeed, modern Ireland is a very scary place for some children and young adults. I am talking about the plight of lone parents, children born into dysfunction and underachievement. There are many obstacles in their way. There are others from families who have the pressures of mounting debt, housing costs, two-job households and latch-door children. Yet some students have designer clothes, mobile phones and iPods. We have well-educated young people with plenty of money and plenty of freedom. There is wastefulness, binge drinking and experimentation with drugs, to name but some issues. Together, at school and in the home we need to encourage young people to take personal responsibility for their own lives. To do this we need to support the children and their families.

There are problems with parenting issues, with exposure to the internet, lack of parental supervision and differences in parenting standards. Clearly schools, therefore, need increasingly to respond to these issues. Meeting the challenges – both those outlined here and those yet to come – will place demands on all parts of the education system.

And yet, for all the problems and cynicism in my daily life, I deal with fine young people, all of whom with support and leadership can make it into adulthood as fine citizens. For some children school is often the best part of the day! They are involved in caring for themselves and others. If you need to build a school in Africa students will respond, organising all sorts of events from sponsored walks to hurling blitzes. If you need to visit the seven nursing homes in the catchment area, students will get there. If you need to get help as a student because you were bullied, you will get support. While anti-social behaviour among teenagers is often in the news, thousands of fantastic young people are active through the President's Award. No doubt we need a new vision for the changing family.

What Should Change?

A number of factors contribute to the capability of children and young people to engage in learning and to make the most of their educational opportunities. These include being able to make good choices and decisions; an understanding of the impact of their actions – 'if I do *this*, predictably and consistently *that* will happen' – and how to influence events; and the ability (and desire) to concentrate, to apply themselves to a task and persevere.

Reports highlight evidence that some children are less likely to have access to experiences that help them to develop these skills and attitudes. Consequently, while activities to promote such development are of value to all children and young people, they are of particular value to certain groups in closing the attainment gap. These skills and attitudes are as important in further and higher education as in the workplace. However, the national curriculum gives them relatively little weight and they are measured, recorded and reported inadequately by national tests and most public examinations. As a result, they are in danger of being neglected by teachers and undervalued by pupils and their parents at a time when they matter more than ever.

Some schools are already succeeding in narrowing the gaps. They are achieving very different outcomes for their pupils compared with other schools with similar pupil profiles. A strategy for closing the gap through personalising learning and creating a caring environment (Care Teams) will therefore draw heavily on solutions adopted in schools where pupils 'buck the trend'. Such solutions may also be drawn from the experience of different types of schools. However, schools cannot be held solely responsible for 'closing the gap'. Schools and homes in communities damaged by generations of underachievement, unemployment and social fragmentation rightly expect other agencies to help them tackle systemic barriers to raising the aspirations of children, parents and teachers.

Local implementation of home and school agendas in contributing to human, social and spiritual development offers the opportunity to improve continuity and progression in learning for children at risk of falling behind. All schools recognise these challenges. Some have identified the potential of personalising learning and employing a caring culture to offer a framework for their response and have set about the task with energy and enthusiasm.

The government's education policy profoundly influences the path and speed of transformation in schools. Some recent important developments have contributed to creating a climate of frustration where little development can take place. There is a great need for:

- The encouragement of greater diversity among schools, with each developing a distinctive ethos in response to local context and in partnership with local stakeholders;
- Interventions designed to tackle the link between disadvantage and poor outcomes for children and young people;
- Increased collaboration between early years settings, between groups of schools, between schools and other educational institutions, and between schools and other organisations;
- Emphasising the role of local communities and parishes as champions of the needs of pupils and parents, in commissioning services for children and young people and in assuring the quality and accessibility of those services;
- Developing and clarifying teachers' and support staff's responsibilities and stressing the importance of high levels

of professionalism among the school workforce, enabling schools to lead change;

- Increasing emphasis on schools' responsibilities for self-evaluation and improvement, and for contributing to gathering and disseminating knowledge about what works.

What Can Change?

We need to continue with true social order but we are fettered by economics and budget cutbacks. Decisions made by schools, national government and agencies in the short-term could and should have a powerful and lasting effect on the character and quality of schooling and parenting in the future. Too many children drift into underachievement and disengagement and fail to make progress in their learning. Pupils need to become more skilled at learning new knowledge and skills, not just what the school offers today. Today's children and young people are less passive, biddable and deferential than in past generations. There have been dramatic advances in the availability and capacity of technology to widen access to, and options for, learning. We should be pioneering and evaluating approaches to learning how to learn. While school is a central feature of the lives of the vast majority of children and young people from the age of five, it is not their first experience of learning. The skills and attitudes they need to become expert learners are shaped from birth. Mothers and fathers are children's first teachers. There is compelling evidence that parental aspirations, expectations and involvement have a major impact on their children's attainment. Parents play a highly significant role in modeling behaviour for their children, including literacy.

None of these require formal structures – they are shown in parents believing (and showing that they believe) in their children's ability to succeed and through 'at home good parenting'.

These factors are not evenly distributed among all parents. Rather, they are associated with family income, social class and levels of education, thereby continuing the disparity of educational experience and outcomes between different groups. However, positive parenting styles can be learned, and breaking the cycle of disadvantage is central to the agenda for social justice. Not all of the factors which have an impact on schools' abilities to engage parents in their children's education will be susceptible to short-term measures. The government, communities and parishes must understand that engaging parents and families in school and community activities is important. Support has been given to the early years: childcare, pre-school education and services for maternal and child health. However, we need to see the introduction of parenting programmes. This includes piloting parent support advisers and establishing the Local Network Groups for Parents.

Schools, supported by other services for children, young people and families, must engage parents in their children's education. Parents should have easy access to information and, where necessary, access to more targeted support. Schools must use their resources to promote the good practices and behaviours that are at the heart of personalising learning and developing caring. These resources include physical resources, such as learning spaces and new technologies, but go beyond them to include the use of time and the way schools make best use of the skills of their pupils, teachers, support staff, parents and other members of the community.

One must ask the question, where are we going and what can we do? Although we have had our share of problems in the past five years we have never suspended or expelled a student. This year we will celebrate the achievement of having the first Traveller qualify as a primary teacher.

How this is achieved / what we should change:

In the home and school relationship we need to spend more time:

- Catching people, young and old, at what they are good at;
- Rewarding good behaviour;
- Appointing a school chaplain to all schools (parish);
- Living out our mission and ethos;
- Developing a sense of the whole school community;
- Developing and improving dialogue for Parent Teacher Student Meetings (PTSM);
- Improving the partnership of learning and teaching through nurturing the parent and home involvement;
- Involving students democratically through the Students' Council;
- Working with limited resources to sustain and support all members of the school community;
- Promoting active home–school dialogue;
- Creating and sharing best practice between schools;
- Using ICT technology to link all partners in the learning and teaching agenda, for example, Moodle.
- Encouraging greater transparency between home and school and vice-versa;
- Offering a hopeful agenda.

The important role played by schools is recognised by the DES:

> Education not only reflects society but also influences its development. As such, schools have a role to play in the development of an intercultural society. While education cannot bear the sole responsibility for challenging racism and promoting intercultural competence, it has an important contribution to make in the development of the child's intercultural skills,

attitudes, values and knowledge. An intercultural education is valuable to all children in equipping them to participate in an increasingly diverse society. Equally, an education which is based on only one culture will be less likely to develop these capacities in children.

Through schools networking and sharing we can promote family/home well-being, resourcefulness and family support. There are implications of the new economic reality for family life. We must move to support changing family patterns. There is no doubt that relationships have suffered, particularly in the area of family and the community at the paws of the Celtic Tiger. The difficult economic experiences of the current climate will no doubt affect the family, home and school even more. Our experience shows that we need to support these children and their families to go through a tough life with dignity. Finally, we are fortunate to live in an Ireland where so many fine people give of their best. Working together, the home and school can create a true social order where every life is important.

Contributors

Fr Harry Bohan, Chairman of the Céifin Centre, qualified as a sociologist in the University of Wales and is currently Director of Pastoral Planning in the Diocese of Killaloe and parish priest in Sixmilebridge, Co. Clare. In 1998 he founded The Céifin Centre for Values-led Change to reflect, debate and direct values-led change in Irish society. He has written extensively on Christianity, spirituality, economic development and on understanding change. His publications include *Ireland Green, Hope Begins at Home* and *Community and the Soul of Ireland*.

Cardinal Seán Brady was educated in St Patrick's College, Maynooth, where he received a BA in Ancient Classics, before moving to Rome where he completed a doctorate in Canon Law in 1967. He was ordained in 1964 and has held various positions since, including Professor of St Patrick's College, Cavan; Vice-Rector and Rector of Irish College, Rome; parish priest of Castletara, Co. Cavan; and, ultimately, Archbishop of Armagh and Primate of All Ireland since 1996. He was made Cardinal by Pope Benedict XVI in November 2007.

Kieran McKeown is a social and economic research consultant. He has carried out research for a diverse range of government departments, statutory agencies and voluntary bodies. Over the past decade, his research has had a major focus on family well-being and the effectiveness of services, including parenting programmes and couple counselling, in supporting families. He has also carried out a range of studies on the mental health needs of children, evaluating the effectiveness of mental health programmes, and researched the prevalence of special education needs among children.

Charles Handy is a writer, broadcaster and lecturer. His books on the changing shape of work and its effects on our lives and organisations have sold almost two million copies worldwide. He has, in his career, been an oil executive, a business economist and a professor at the London Business School. He is also known for his *Thought for Today* on the BBC Radio breakfast show, *Today*. He was born in Ireland and grew up in Kildare, but now lives in London. A copy of his autobiography, *Myself and Other More Important Matters*, was given to each delegate at the conference.

Elizabeth Handy has been pursuing a dual career since 1990, as business partner to her writer husband Charles and as an independent portrait photographer. In her photography she has experimented with her new form of portraiture of 'still lifes'. She has also developed a 'joiner' technique, in which she combines the different roles of an individual or a family in one composite portrait. It is this technique that she has used in her Families Project. Examples of her work can be seen by visiting her website at www.lizhandy.net.

Dr John Yzaguirre has been a keynote speaker at international and national conventions in the United States, Canada, Mexico and Europe in areas of family life, prosocial skills development and cross-cultural issues. He is a licensed psychologist, educator and author. Besides his active private practice and speaking engagements, he works as a consultant to business, educational, religious and health organisations throughout the United States. With his wife, Claire Frazier-Yzaguirre, MFT, M.Div., he has co-authored the book, *Thriving Marriages: An Inspirational and Practical Guide to Lasting Happiness*.

Ciana Campbell, originally from Swinford, Co. Mayo, has a BA in Psychology. She began her broadcasting career in RTÉ in 1980. For the following eighteen years, Ciana presented and reported on both radio and television. She was the recipient of a number of awards, including a Jacob's Television Award and an A.T. Cross Woman Journalist Award. She provides media consultancy, training and presentation services to a variety of organisations. In 2006 she was awarded a Higher Diploma in Health Promotion by NUIG. Ciana lives with her family in Ennis, Co. Clare.

Mamo McDonald became well known for her leadership of the Irish Countrywomen's Association in the 1980s. She has been working on ageing issues since 1987, when she chaired Ireland's first National Day of Ageing – an initiative that led to the setting up of Age & Opportunity, of which she was Chairperson until 2001 and is now Honorary President. Her leadership of the organisation won her a People of the Year award in 1999. At age seventy she embarked on a Higher Diploma in Women's Studies, and now holds a Masters Degree in the same subject.

Kevin Murphy has been a stay-at-home dad for the past twelve years. Previously a financial journalist with the *Irish Independent*, he lives in Dublin with his three teenage children and wife, Gina Quin, Chief Executive of the Dublin Chamber of Commerce. He has been a regular contributor on national radio and television, including The Marian Finucane Show, David McWilliams' Big Byte and The Pat Kenny Show. Kevin is qualified in Psychology, Investment & Treasury and Psychoanalytic Psychotherapy and is a practicing psychotherapist. He is author of *It's A Dad's Life*, a book about being a stay-at-home parent.

Geraldine Reidy was born in Limerick and emigrated to Canada in 1974, where she lived for twenty-two years. She attended Queens University, Kingston, Ontario, where she studied Sociology and English. While in Canada she worked in the community sector, working closely with wives and families of inmates in Kingston, Ontario. Geraldine returned to Ireland in 1996 and currently works in a community setting in Limerick. She is a member of OPEN, a national organisation for one-parent families. She is also a trained facilitator in the Strengthening Families – Strengthening Communities Programme, introduced to Ireland by OPEN.

Jim Power is a graduate of University College, Dublin. He is Chief Economist at Friends First Group. He previously worked as Chief Economist at Bank of Ireland Group and Treasury Economist at AIB Group. He teaches Finance and Economics on the Local Government MBA at Dublin City University and Economics on the Executive MBA at the Michael Smurfit Graduate School of Business in Ireland. He writes a weekly column in the *Irish Examiner* and is the editor of the Friends First *Quarterly Economic Outlook*, which has become established as one of Ireland's leading commentaries on the Irish economy.

Geoffrey Shannon is a solicitor and senior lecturer in family and child law at the Law Society of Ireland. He also holds various other positions, such as Special Rapporteur for Child Protection, Irish Expert Member of the Commission on

European Family Law and Chairman of the Adoption Board of Ireland. He is a prolific author, with his most recent book being a major new work on divorce, entitled *Divorce: Law and Practice* (Thompson Round Hall, 2008). He is also the editor of the *Irish Journal of Family Law* and has written extensively on family and child law issues.

Marie Murray has worked as a Clinical Psychologist since 1975. She is a Director of the Student Counselling Services in University College Dublin, prior to which she was Director of Psychology at St Vincent's Psychiatric Hospital in Dublin. She is an *Irish Times* health columnist and a well-known contributor to radio and television; she may be known best for her years providing a weekly psychology slot on the *Today with Pat Kenny* radio programme. The hardback edition of Marie's most recent book, *Living Our Times*, sold out immediately and is now available in paperback.

John Quinn was a senior producer with RTÉ Radio 1 from 1977 to 2002. His programmes won numerous distinctions, including three Jacobs Awards, and his weekly educational magazine, *The Open Mind*, ran for thirteen years. A former teacher at both primary and post-primary levels, he also spent five years as an editor in educational publishing. He has written six novels, five for children, one of which won a Bisto Children's Book of the Year Award. His most recent book, *Goodnight Ballivor, I'll Sleep in Trim*, a childhood memoir, was published by Veritas in 2008.

Mary Forde is Principal of Presentation College, Athenry, Co. Galway. She has a wide range of experience of the Irish education system, having worked on secondment to the Department of Education & Science for twelve years. She was involved with both writing and developing the very successful

Leaving Certificate Vocational Programme (LCVP), and currently works with the DES in the training of school principals at second level. She was responsible for a number of innovations in the Irish education system and currently works with a Professional Learning Network on the sharing of best practice in Irish second level education.

Tracking the Tiger

A Decade of Change

This set of papers sets out to recall and trace what has been happening in key areas of Irish life over the last decade. It explores the influence of the economic miracle, and the values which have shaped us throughout.

978 184730 090 4
€12.95

Freedom: Licence or Liberty?

Engaging with a transforming Ireland

There is little dispute that Ireland in the twenty-first century is a society in transformation. With an economy registering unparalleled growth, a rising population buoyed by an enriching immigrant community and an overall confidence in our future, we have much to celebrate. There is, however, a downside to that transformation. We may, by some criteria, be deemed the second wealthiest nation in the world, but for all our success there are many who feel disconnected and marginalised in our society. We may be free from the shackles – economic or social – of our past, but does that freedom constitute true liberty or is it engendering a licence that is ultimately threatening the fabric of our 'new' society?

978 1 84730 028 7 • €14.95

Filling the Vacuum?

The Céifin Centre for Values-Led Change is about holding a mirror up to the reality of modern society. Based in Shannon, it has been doing this in different ways since its foundation in 1998. One of these ways is through its annual conference, which now attracts over 500 people from a cross-section of Irish society and is the focus of widespread media coverage.

Despite our increasing prosperity, there is a growing sense of isolation and disconnectedness in Irish society. For that reason the theme 'filling the vacuum' was chosen for Conference 2005. What interventions are needed to establish and promote a strong sense of belonging within our society? This was a particularly successful conference, very well attended, with excellent presentations and lively feedback from the floor. These presentations are now contained in this publication and make compelling reading for those of us working towards a better society.

978 1 85390 947 4

€12.95

Imagining the Future

Ireland as a society is in a unique position at this moment in time. Over the last ten years our standard of living has increased, while at the same time our belief in state and religious institutions has dwindled. However, the issue of how to relate to one another and to the wider world is only beginning to be explored, as is the issue of becoming a multi-cultural society.

Contributors include Archbishop Diarmuid Martin, Emily O'Reilly (Ireland's Ombudsman), Michael D. Higgins, Catherine Byrne (the Deputy General Secretary of the Irish National Teachers' Organisation), Mike Cooley (Chairman of the Joint EU/India Scientific Committee and a chief consultant to the UN on technological impacts) and Tina Roche (Chief Executive of The Foundation for Investing in Communities).

978 1 85390 804 0

€12.95

Global Aspirations and the Reality of Change
How can we do things differently?

Just imagine experiencing a feast of stories, ideas, dialogue, music, drama and good conversation …

Just imagine being transported through the revolution that Ireland has experienced in the past decade – the rise and rise in consumption, the acceleration in the pace of work and personal life, the effect of communication replacing transmission, the means overcoming the end … but despite all that, imagine that change is possible. Imagine a revolution of deceleration.

'Indifference will not be allowed': imagine the challenge of these five words!

Just imagine having a whole morning to reflect on the possibilities of influencing the system of power that keeps us politically docile and economically productive. Imagine the joy of realising that power is present in every moment, in every relationship and there is ultimately no 'small act'.

Just imagine all that and the camaraderie and the energy of spending two days with three hundred people who want to do things differently, who want to effect change. Imagine conversations – at early and late hours – stories, dreams, ideas, debate, energy.

978 1 85390 742 5 • €13.95

Values and Ethics   Can I make a difference?

What are the values that we choose to prioritise and live by? What price are we prepared to pay for ethics? Is it enough to rely on the law as the minimum standard of acceptable behaviour? Ultimately, can one person make a difference?

These and other far-reaching questions are addressed in *Values and Ethics,* the fifth collection of papers from the Céifin Conference which is held annually in Ennis, Co. Clare. Contributors include Professor Robert Putnam (author of *Bowling Alone*), sociologist Dr Tony Fahey, Bishop Willie Walsh and Dr Lorna Gold from the University of York.

There is a belief in Ireland that we have not adjusted to our new-found prosperity. In a society that measures almost everything in monetary terms, values and ethics are increasingly sidelined. We now face the challenge of taking our social growth as seriously as we take our economic growth.

This book gives hope that real change can begin with committed individuals who believe passionately that shared values can become a social reality.

978 1 85390 658 9 • €13.95

Is The Future My Responsibility?

Have we become helpless in the face of change or can
we manage the future? More and more people talk
about the emptiness of modern life; they wonder where
meaning is coming from and what values are shaping us;
they say it is not easy being young today in spite of the
choices and the freedom. We cannot assume that if we
simply sit back and comment the storm will blow over,
or that we will return to the old ways. The fact is we are
experiencing a cultural transformation, we are
witnessing the passing of a tradition, the end of an era.
Every day we hear questions like 'Why aren't they doing
something about it?' or 'Who is responsible for this,
that or the other?' It is time to ask: 'Have I got any
responsibility for the way things are?'

Including contributions from Nobel Laureate John Hume and internationally
renowned writer and broadcaster Charles Handy, *Is the Future My
Responsibility?* is the fourth book of papers from the Céifin conference, held
annually in Ennis, County Clare, and published by Veritas.

978 1 85390 605 3 • €12.50

Redefining Roles and Relationships?

*These annual conferences in Ennis are establishing
themselves as an important date in the calendar and
meeting a need for serious discussion about major social
and ethical issues of the day.*

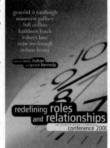

Mary Robinson
United Nations High Commissioner for Human Rights

The papers presented at the third Ennis Conference
in 2000 are collected in this book. The need to
redefine roles and relationships in a rapidly changing
society was examined in many areas of modern life.

Papers include: 'Contemplating Alternative
Relationships of Power in a Historical Perspective', Gearóid Ó Tuathaigh;
'Rebuilding Social Capital: Restoring an Ethic of Care in Irish Society',
Maureen Gaffney; 'Rise of Science, Rise of Atheism: Challenge to Christianity',
Bill Collins; 'Social Justice and Equality in Ireland', Kathleen Lynch; 'Putting
People at the Centre of Things', Robert E. Lane; 'Why Are We Deaf to the
Cry of the Earth?', Seán McDonagh; 'It's Just the Media', Colum Kenny.

978 1 85390 562 9 • €11.40

Working Towards Balance

There is growing consensus that corporate and market values now shape Irish society.

Economic growth is synonymous with progress. But economic activity represents only one facet of human existence. Its values are not the only values that prevail in society. As we begin a new millennium, our society must be challenged to wonder what direction it is taking. There is an obvious need to ensure that the agenda of the corporate world and the welfare of local communities can co-exist in a meaningful relationship.

These are the concerns that were addressed at the 'Working Towards Balance' conference in 1999, organised by Rural Resource Development Ltd (now the Céifin Centre), the papers of which are published in this book.

978 1 85390 474 5 • €11.40

Are we forgetting something?

'Romantic Ireland's dead and gone, it's with O'Leary in the grave', was the poet's cry a century ago. On the cusp of the third millennium many people fear the death of the Irish sense of community. The concept of a caring society seems well-buried in the selfishness of consumerism and *mé-féin*-ism encouraged by the phenomenon of the Celtic Tiger.

These were the concerns that inspired Fr Harry Bohan to organise a conference on the theme 'Are We Forgetting Something? Our Society in the New Millennium' in November 1998. Topics addressed ranged from the human search for meaning, to the economic boom in context.

This provocative and incisive volume, ably edited by Harry Bohan and Gerard Kennedy, also includes the views of the three chairpersons of the conference: Marie Martin, John Quinn and Michael Kenny, and is interspersed with well-chosen poetic and spiritual reflections on the topics addressed.

978 1 85390 457 8 • €11.40